# Dreama Kay

A Memoir

PAMELA MEADOWS-GOMEZ

ISBN: 978-1-965679-85-2 (sc)
ISBN: 978-1-965679-86-9 (e)

Rev. date: 04/09/2025

# Dedication

For you, Patty, from me, with love

# Contents

# Acknowledgments

Our sincere thanks to St. Josephs's Hospital in Ann Arbor, Michigan and Medilodge Convalescent Home in Howell, Michigan. We are all grateful for your efforts in comforting our sister, Patty, and all of us as well. Medilodge was incredibly generous, not just with their time, but with food, accommodations, and, most importantly, their genuine love and caring for all of us in those days. All of you will remain in our hearts forever.

I would also like to thank my sisters and brothers. This traumatic event has brought us all closer; however, this book revisits many deep, dark areas of our past. Each of us has our own way of dealing with it, and I recognize that I'm asking my siblings to accept that our private past will now become much more public. Please know I am extremely appreciative of all of you.

I also need to thank my sister, Jackie. She's the person I talked with about every aspect of this book. She lent an ear and an opinion, and she stayed silent when I was adamant about keeping in, or taking out, some parts. This book may have been written without her, but it's so much better because of her.

Finally, I need to thank my own family. Reliving moments, both past and present, has been a heart-wrenching, emotionally draining experience for me, and I appreciate their patience as I wrote, rewrote, set aside, and brought back out this labor of love for a beautiful, loving, inspiring sister. Thank you, Patty. While your life's spirit continues to live on, I hope this book ensures your life's legacy will as well.

# Introduction

As I begin writing this book, Patty (Dreama Kay) is still alive. When Patty was young, she always said she wished Mom had named her "Dreama Kay." She loved that name, and we all thought she'd name her daughter that, but she decided on Buffy, which is unique and different. Patty had wanted that name only for herself, which made perfect sense to me.

Diagnosed days ago with brain cancer, Patty's battle to live has begun in earnest. She has been told she could have a year to live. They are preparing her for radiation, which they will begin in a few days. This book will be my way to cope, and wait, until Jackie, my younger sister, and I go home to Michigan from California two weeks from now. I vacillate between wanting to grab a plane right now, with my dirty shirt and boxers on, and running fast and far in the other direction, because I do not want my sister to die.

Let this be the way I've chosen to allow others to understand how things really were and how those things set the stage for so many other things to happen to Patty and to all of us. I wanted to wait until my parents died to write about out childhoods, but life-or perhaps death-has intervened. Watching my parents display genuine emotion for Patty makes me certain I won't be able to write the truth after they are gone. It also makes me wonder why they couldn't have expressed these emotions long, long ago. I have written several books; however, they are mostly about child abuse. This is a new area for me, but I need a way to deal with what is happening right now. I am so frustrated that I cannot be there right this second to help them all. They need it.

I have changed the names of some people in this book. I wanted to change mine too. This book is mostly my memory only; it is my perspective on our childhoods and current lives. It will probably be pretty close to the truth, as over the years we've shared many of the same stories. Yes, I am prone to exaggerate a bit. Big lizards have been called snakes, etc., but this is real life, and unfortunately, there is no need to enhance, embellish, or flat-out lie. The truth is frightening, disgusting, unbelievably sad, frustrating, hellish, nightmarish, and, occasionally, loving and moving. I hope to strike a balance in there and write not just about the sad, maddening parts but the others as well. It will be a challenge, though, because I always remember back and feel gut-wrenching, heart-wrenching anger. I will try to temper those feelings with some real, genuinely nice moments. Though it didn't happen often, we did laugh and love as brothers and sisters.

While everyone's days are numbered, it is horrifyingly frightening when the countdown begins...

Just as Jackie and I were preparing ourselves and our mom to go to Michigan, I got the call at work. It was my older sister Connie. She was crying. The hospital in Ann Arbor had done more tests on Patty, and they found a malignant tumor in her esophagus. The doctors decided that it would be no use to try radiation on her. The cancer in her brain was moving rapidly; there was nothing left to do. The doctors gave her a week to live.

*What? No! No!* They had just told us a few days ago she had a year. This cannot be so. I was teaching when Connie called, and I told her that Jackie and I would go to Michigan the next day. Connie had just left Michigan and returned to her home in Atlanta, and then she received this horrible news. She would be making a return trip to Michigan also. I do not know how I got through that day. I teach physical education at a middle school, and my dear friend Norma, who is my assistant, walked me through the necessary steps for me to leave. I told Frank, Joel, and Quinn, the teachers I work with, and I knew they would take care of things here for me. I called Jackie, who was clearly distraught, and we quickly began to make plans.

We would not be able to take Mom. Mom has been living in this skilled-care facility for almost five years, and the nurses and doctors there needed time to prepare her for this trip. We didn't know how to tell her she couldn't come; we'd already told her we were planning to take her in two weeks. Our mom takes several medications that she needs every single day, and without them, she would suffer. We knew this would be terribly hard for everyone, especially for the person who had brought Patty into the world.

Dad knew he couldn't come; he'd had several strokes a few years back, and he is bedridden. He cannot move his entire right side, and much of his left side has begun to atrophy. He has been told, like Mom, that Patty is very sick and we need to leave immediately. Jackie and I have decided we will wait until we come home to tell them. They really cannot do anything right now to help, and it would only cause them to worry more.

# Jackie

Jackie (Jacka, Goob, Goober) is the youngest of the five girls. Mom had us five girls first, Linda, Patty, Connie, me and Jackie, followed by three boys, JayJay, Gary, and Darryl.

This is the only picture we have of all
of us when we were young
From back left: Mom, Dad, Linda.
From middle left: Jackie, Patty, Connie
From front left: Gary, JayJay, Darryl
(standing sideways-Connie has her
hand on his shoulder), and Me.

Jackie and I are actually only eleven months apart. I always say that's because Mom and Dad were so thrilled with me they couldn't wait to try for another one. Of course, the reality is that there weren't good forms of birth control back then. I think in those days women just sort of acquiesced to whatever men wanted.

Jackie and I grew up very close. We were so much alike. We liked the same boys at church—usually only when the other one liked him—and we were always sharing stories about how far we'd gone with boys. That's when the baseball diamond was used as a gauge to determine your level of sexual activity. It almost became a race between us to see which one would lose their virginity first. Frankly, I don't remember who won; I know it was a close race.

Jackie's inquisitiveness as a child was very different from mine, though. I wanted everything to stay exactly the same, and I didn't want to know what was beyond anywhere. She was a young child when she had her stomach pumped after she ate a bottle of baby aspirin. In her defense, they did taste good-kind of like a Sweet Tart. Some time later, she ate a box of Ex-Lax, but I think that time her stomach pumped it out. Jackie, the nonbeliever, asked, "Are you sure if I put my tongue on this frozen tree, with icicles hanging from it, that my tongue will freeze and the top layer of my tongue will get ripped off? Yes, we are sure.

Gosh, that scared the heck out of me. Jackie and I were waiting for the school bus. It was so cold that day, and when I looked at her, her tongue was stuck on the tree! I screamed for Mom, and she came running outside. Jackie had pried her tongue from the tree, and blood was everywhere! Just then, the bus came. I remember Mom telling me to get on the bus and that she'd be okay, but I worried about her all day. Mom was right, but what a scare.

Jackie spent about six months with our aunt Judy and uncle Lemuel when she was young, and I know she had a great time. They cared for her and bought her whatever she needed, and they mostly just let her know that she was loved. We missed her, though. I remember the day she came back home. JayJay and I stood on top of the garage, waiting to see their car come around the curve. We jumped up and down when they got to the house. For at least a whole day, everyone was nice to Jackie, and we all told her how happy we were she was home. Then we all returned to our normal lives, fighting with each other all the time.

Ironically, as close as Jackie and I were, when the girls fought, the lines were drawn well in advance. It was Patty and me versus Jackie and Connie. They were never physical; the fights were just verbal sparring. Nobody really ever won. Or at least if we lost, I cannot, or will not, recall it. Jackie got married at seventeen. She graduated six months earlier than her classmates, and she decided she wanted to marry Roger. It was a very special day. In those years, Mom was able to function very well. and she sewed most of the bridesmaids' dresses. Jackie looked beautiful, and Roger looked very handsome. He was our neighbor up the street, so we all knew him and his family. Roger was a genuinely nice guy.

Almost immediately, though, they moved to Rantoul, Illinois. Roger had enlisted in the air force, and he was ultimately stationed there. Roger had enlisted before discussing it with Jackie, and she was terribly upset about it, with good reason.

While living in Illinois, Jackie met Bob. She had divorced Roger, and she and Bob began dating. Together, they left Illinois and moved to California. I followed a few years later after a bad relationship breakup. I stayed with them for a month (I virtually had nothing but my car and a few belongings), and then I moved into a furnished apartment close by them. We had many fun, wonderful times. They were amazing pool players, and they also played darts.

Jackie is an incredible businesswoman. She can take a business and twist it and turn it and make it make money. She has worked for some top department stores, and she knows a lot about style and fashion. She has long since given up on me, however.

"Jackie, I am not going to pull everything out of my black purse just because I'm wearing all brown!"

She is also a great cook and a wonderful aunt. When she first married Bob, I always told her she should have a child with him. After I had my three children, Jackie kept them and continues to keep them in the best designer clothes and shoes, and she loves them more than anything, so I just shut up. Jackie currently manages a department store here in California. She divorced Bob several years ago, and she and her boyfriend Steve live just a few minutes from us. No one knows me as well as she does. She always knows what I'm going to do, usually before I do it. We have always been close. Jackie and I will be a little better off than our other siblings; we have each other.

We step out of the rental car, and Jackie and I start walking toward the biggest building. This place is huge, and we aren't sure we are in the right place. My cell phone rings; I hear Patty's daughter Buffy's voice, and she says she is walking toward us. We see Loretta, my oldest sister Linda's daughter, coming toward us too. All of us start running until the four of us are hugging and sobbing. Our sweet little Buffy looks exhausted, and Loretta looks so scared.

We walk together into Patty's room. Roger, Buffy's husband, is there, and Linda and her husband, Rich, are there too. They all share the same look of impending something—I will not say impending death.

# Linda

Linda (Belinda) is our oldest sister. Mom had Linda when she was sixteen, at home, in West Virginia. Linda taught us how to shimmy, do the mashed potato, tease our hair, and why we shouldn't get pregnant at sixteen. Linda was married to Ron. Well, she was pregnant with our nephew Ronnie at sixteen, and in those days, you just got married.

Ronnie was just the most adorable boy! Patty and I babysat Ronnie when he was young because Ron and Linda worked at a factory together. We were young ourselves, but we enjoyed him so much. He got his first stitches with us. We let him stand on a chair with no back, and he fell; he got four stitches on the chin. And I am personally responsible for teaching him how to French kiss! He was about eighteen months old, and I was bored that day. Linda was so mad at me when I told Ronnie to give his mommy a big kiss, and he slid his little tongue in there too!

We had so much fun with Ron too. When we were young and he was dating Linda, he'd pack us all in his car and take us to the A&W. They'd bring the trays over and attach them to the window, and we would eat in the car. Those moments helped us get through the other moments. He always made us feel that he cared about us.

We gave him the scare of his life too. One Sunday, he took a bunch of us to Walkerville, a small store a few miles from our church, so we could get some penny candy. Well, we always asked Ron to "peel out" no matter where we were. He usually would do it for us (not at church, though). We all packed into the car, and Ron thought we were all in. He peeled out! It was great except that Connie's door wasn't shut all the way, and she fell halfway out of the car. He didn't know it, but he was dragging her as he drove! We all started screaming, but Ron thought it was because he had peeled out. He finally stopped the car and got out. His face was ashen; Linda was scared to death too. Connie was badly scratched up everywhere on her body, it seemed, and she was crying hard. That was unusual for her because she was so tough, and she seldom ever cried. The rest of us were crying too because we almost fell out as well. Ron and Linda were both relieved when Connie stood up and started walking. They were surprised, though, when, instead of walking toward the car, she began walking toward the store.

"Where are you going? "Ron asked.

"My candy fell out. I'm going back to get it!"

Linda had a nice singing voice. She sang "Tom Dooley" at a 4-H talent show one year, but she didn't win because Tom Dooley had killed someone, and the song itself was deemed inappropriate by the 4-H judges. It turns out Connie and Patty were somewhat disqualified too. They did a little dance routine to Elvis's "All Shook Up." While it was incredibly tame, even by their strict standards, they didn't win either.

Linda sang in a band at a local bar for a while. She is a talented singer, but it generally takes opportunity, luck, or something that Linda didn't get to take your career to another level.

We were involved in an accident when brother JayJay was a baby. The roads were a solid sheet of ice, and our car spun and spun, and it finally hit a tree. We were all jolted, but JayJay, who was just a few months old, went through the windshield. The back of his head was cut very badly, and Mom and Dad had to take him to get stitches. We stayed with some friends who lived nearby, and she let us make sugar doughnuts to take our mind off Jayjay. It worked; they were delicious! JayJay carries a long scar down the back of his head to this day, which is another good reason why he wears his hair in a ponytail.

Linda hit her head during the accident, and shortly afterward, she began to have seizures. Her body jerked violently, her eyes rolled back in her head, and we always believed she was going to swallow her tongue. In those days, doctors thought it was possible too. Mom was told to grab a spoon, force her mouth open, and hold her tongue down. Mom made sure we watched what she did so we would also know what to do if it happened and she wasn't there. She would hold her tongue down until the seizure passed. It seemed to take forever. She had grand mal seizures. Linda would be exhausted after those episodes; she would sometimes sleep for twenty-four hours. The medications she took helped tremendously, however, and eventually the seizures became a rarity for her. You would think that after a while you would become a bit desensitized to them, but the last one I saw Linda have freaked me out as much as the first one. There is something incredibly frightening about watching a person's body react in such a way.

Loretta, who was born four years after Ronnie, also had some seizures when she was an infant. She was fortunate, though; they lasted for a short time and never returned. Loretta was an absolute delight. She was sweet, loving, and beautiful. We all just loved to see her smile at us. When we were young, we just couldn't believe something that beautiful had come out of our sister!

She is a hard worker. Her parents were farmers; she had many chores, just as Ronnie did. Ron taught Ronnie how to coon hunt, and he taught him all about farming. We were, and continue to be, proud of them both. Loretta would help clean bulk tanks, make coffee and food, along with many other things, from a very early age. Linda had gained quite a bit of weight throughout this time. She decided she was going to lose it, and she did! She lost close to one hundred pounds by using willpower alone. She also went back and got her GED. Our entire family was extremely proud of her.

Linda and Ron divorced after many years of marriage. They'd been so young, and farming is a 24/7 job that can absolutely consume everyone; even the children had their jobs to help keep the farm running. We also saw Ron when we were home. He hadn't changed a bit. Jackie and I just enjoyed catching up and spending a moment with him. He had also remarried, and he now had four young sons (from his new wife's previous marriage), so he was very busy.

Unfortunately, Linda developed type 2 diabetes, and she struggles with it to this day. She has been on dialysis for six years, and it has taken its toll. She also suffers from osteoporosis, which compromises her in many ways as well. So, on the days she has dialysis, she arrives late in the afternoon, but she and Rich, her second husband, always come. They live in Flint, which is an hour's drive to Ann Arbor for them.

Jackie and I met Rich when we went home for Buffy's wedding in 1998. He is a nice guy who clearly loves Linda very much. Rich and Linda have some classic cars that they have put in car shows. They are very active people, which is really good for them both.

Ronnie, Ron and Linda's son, has a daughter, Kaylee, whom we've not met; she is young, maybe twelve or thirteen now. Ronnie married a wonderful woman, JoAnn. She is sweet, down-to-earth, and extremely cordial. I look at Ronnie, and I want to smile. He still has those beautiful, kind eyes and a great smile. Ronnie was our first; we all fell in love with him.

Loretta married and had a son, Trevor, who is about eleven now. She and her husband divorced, and she added another son, Patrick, who is two years old. Loretta still works very hard, and most of the time, she works more than one job. She is so beautiful on the inside and outside, and she can always make us laugh with her matter-of-fact, straightforward way of life. Linda and Ron must be so very proud to have raised such good, hardworking children.

I am sitting in your hospital room. We have begun the death vigil. I so want them to try radiation, or chemotherapy, or a magic elixir, or I want to take you to the river of miracles. I cannot believe you are leaving this world; it cannot be so—you, who have worked so hard and struggled so desperately in every aspect of your life. It isn't fair. And while life isn't always fair, shouldn't there be some balance in the universe, some justice to be meted out? I am grateful that you have acknowledged me; you called me "smartass." I cannot tell you how good that made me feel. You smiled too. I had no illusions about what to expect, and that is a good thing.

Poor Buffy and Brad. It has always been the three of you, and now there will be just the two. Roger loves you so much, Patty. He is a blessing to us all. I knew it eight years ago, and I am reminded of it constantly. He is Buffy's rock, strong, brave, and courageous right now.

I am so glad we learned about God and Jesus when we were young. I know God is calling you, but we are too. Sometimes I get so mad at myself for being so optimistic, but right now it's all I've got. If God chose to, he could heal you this second, the next second, or the next.

I wonder what you are thinking right now. The morphine and Haldol must be really messing with your thought processes. Do you know or understand what is happening to you? The last you knew, they were about to start radiation. Are you preparing in some way to go? I am thankful that I am able to be here; it is where I belong.

It is morning now. I stayed with you last night, Patty, and you had a very rough time. It is heartbreaking to see you this way and to not be able to help you. Today I find myself asking God if he's not going to heal you, to take you quickly. I haven't shared this with anyone yet, but last night, over your bed, I saw something that looked like white sparkling dust coming down from the ceiling. It was glittery, floating, and kind of hovering over you. I looked twice because I couldn't believe it was truly there. But it was. Your special guardian angel is here, in this room, waiting.

Patty, you have never been a quitter. You are a fighter, through and through. I bring this up for several reasons. I vividly remember you stepping between Mom and Dad's screaming matches and telling them to stop acting like kids and to grow up. It actually worked once, but most of the time, it didn't. At least you tried. One of my favorite memories of you is not one isolated incident. It is what you did for me over a long period of time. I always had nightmares, the same recurring nightmares, and they were unbelievably scary. Because our parents fought so violently and frequently, even nights when they didn't fight, I would have nightmares. I would always see the whole house tipping over and everyone falling around, dying. It was very disturbing, mostly because I felt like I couldn't help anyone. I just watched them die, one by one. So, every night you would put your arm around me and sing and rock me to sleep. If you didn't, I couldn't sleep. I don't remember how long you did it, but I remember when the nightmares first started. I was five; you were eight.

Probably the saddest thing in the world to me is that Dad has never admitted what he did to Mom—to all of us. In fact, he would become livid when my husband, Mario, would mention it. Mario had asked him why he used to beat Mom up, and his face turned red and he would yell and sputter his defenses. He had a million excuses, such as it was self-defense and lots of other stuff, but the truth is, the truth is the truth.

The sound of those fights grips my heart and stomach to this day. We'd all be upstairs, and Mom and Dad would be downstairs. First, you would hear them in low, hushed tones. Before long the voices became louder and louder. We always knew when he was about to blow. He would suddenly scream out that he was going to get his gun and kill Mom. We would run down the stairs, trying to pull Mom out of the house. Each time, we'd have a plan in place long before it actually happened. And we needed to change it frequently so that Dad wouldn't know what we were doing. Some of us would take Mom one way to one of our neighbor's homes, and the rest would be either decoys or would try to dissuade Dad from trying to kill Mom. Dad would go for the shotgun every time as we shielded, shoved, and guided Mom outside and away from him. While that horrific ordeal should have been enough, sometimes he would sit on the porch with a loaded shotgun in hand and wait. Imagine being in nightclothes in Michigan's bitterly cold winter with no shoes on, your feet in mounds of snow, and too frightened to move. Long into the night, we'd wait in the field until it was deemed safe to go back in. We knew exactly when too. Dad would just get up, replace the shotgun in the rack, and calmly go to bed.

Jackie and I picked up Gary tonight from the airport. He had fallen off a roof in Houston, where he lives, and he'd had surgery the day before. His ankle was busted up pretty badly, and he was in a lot of pain. But we were so glad to have him with us. We were fortunate to have a hotel room inside the hospital, so Gary was able to see Patty often while we were there. St. Joseph's had provided us with a wheelchair for Gary, which helped immensely.

# Gary

Gary Steven (Bucky, Bucky Beaver, Stevie) is the next-to-youngest brother. Gary, I am sure, never remembered this story, but it is true. One day, when he was a baby, Mom took all of us, and we went to her friend's house several miles away. We played with her kids, and we had fun. When we returned in the early afternoon, though, all hell broke loose. Mom's friend was in the car with us too, and we watched Dad come storming out of the house. He ran to the car and swung the passenger-side door open, where Mom was sitting, holding Gary. He literally grabbed Gary, who was about six weeks old, and threw him about ten feet. We all screamed and cried; it happened so fast that no one could have stopped it. Fortunately, Dad threw him. into our big lilac bush, and except for a few scratches, Gary wasn't hurt badly. Mom and her friend kept telling Dad that nothing had happened and that they had just visited while we played, but he was absolutely livid.

I will never, ever forget what he did next, as I'm sure my mom and siblings won't either. He grabbed Mom out of the car as we begged and pleaded for him not to hurt her. He had a wild-eyed look, and he refused to listen to anyone, including Mom's friend. Then, as we watched in horror, he ripped off every stitch of our mother's clothing, even her panties. He was a damn lunatic, and we were helpless to stop him. Mom's friend was crying hysterically too, and Mom continued trying to reason with him, but it was useless. While our mom stood there in the middle of the afternoon in our front yard, completely naked, Dad bent down and picked up her clothes, and he calmly walked inside the house. Mom followed to put on some clothes, and Mom's friend took off as fast as she could.

We held Gary, trying to assure ourselves he was okay. We'd watched him get flung out of a car; we thought he'd die any second. Dad came storming out of the house with Mom on his heels, screaming at him. He had in his arms every single piece of clothing our mom owned. He didn't say a word. He went straight to the incinerator, and he dropped everything in. Then he pulled out his lighter. They burned so quickly that we barely had time to react. We were yelling and pulling at him, trying desperately to make him understand she'd done nothing wrong. I remember Mom standing there in what she'd found to put on before he'd grabbed everything; she was sobbing. There was nothing left but ashes. Mom's clothes were all gone.

At that moment, I wanted my dad to die. He had humiliated my mom for nothing. Furthermore, no matter if she had done something, he had no right to touch her things, especially since she worked just like he did; in fact, she worked much harder. Mom watched Gary very closely for several days, and she somehow managed to find a few things to wear. I know that none of us ever looked at that lilac bush the same way again, ever.

Not long after that incident, a neighbor friend's husband died. They were destitute. They'd been living in a chicken coop, and the woman was filthy. Mom brought her to our house, and she fed her. That woman ate with such pleasure and gratitude that it made all of us kids feel sorry for her. As the funeral approached, Mom did something I will never forget. She had so few clothes herself, thanks to Dad burning them all, but she gave this lady the only dress she owned. It was not the only time we saw our mother give so willingly, but this was a true example of what a compassionate and giving person our mom was.

Wild and crazy—that was Gary! He was a boy who deliberately did things to scare or hurt us. Yes, that child was mean. He would chase us with hoes and rakes when he was mad, and we never tested him to find out if he was teasing or if he'd actually hit us. To give you an idea of how Gary would exact revenge, here is this story: When Gary was three years old, Linda knocked him off the front porch. Whether it was intentional or not, his top two baby teeth were knocked out. His two permanent teeth did not grow back in for at least five years. And he was very angry about that. So, he waited for the opportune moment. Then one day, when Linda was sitting in front of a window, he saw his chance. He shoved her through the glass, and she fell out onto the grass. She wasn't badly hurt. Our brother got into so much trouble for that, but he just laughed it off, saying, "That's what she gets!"

Gary used to get Mom so mad. When Dad finally built an indoor bathroom for us (I was eight), he put a lock on the inside, but he also put a lock on the outside of the door (I know, I know, we don't know either!). Well, one day while Mom was cleaning Darryl's diapers in the bathroom, Gary locked her in. She was in the house alone with Darryl and Gary, and she yelled and yelled for him to open the door. He just kept laughing. She got even angrier when she kicked the door because, as she brought her foot back, it landed in the bucket of dirty diapers! Thankfully, a man came to the door selling something, and Mom yelled for him to come in and unlock the door.

Mom was furious with Gary for doing that, so she took him outside, where there was a spike nail in one of the trees in the yard. It was low enough for her to hang him up there and high enough that he couldn't touch the ground. She'd teach him a lesson, she thought. When we got home from school several hours later, he was still hanging on the nail, laughing.

Gary had a big cyst on his knee when he was two that had to be removed, and he'd have to stay in the hospital for a few days. The day after the surgery, Mom went to see him, and she saw some frantic nurses. They couldn't find Gary! He couldn't walk because of the surgery. Where could he have gone? Mom went to the crib, and she followed a path out of the room and down the hall, where she could hear a television playing. The nurses had no idea how he'd gotten out of the crib, but he had hobbled on one leg down to the TV room, and he was calmly sitting, watching cartoons.

Gary was an absolute daredevil. Do not dare him to do anything ever. He climbed up on the roof one day; he was probably about ten then. Some neighbors were over, and several of them were trying to coax Gary to jump. We kept telling him not to, that he would get hurt, that it was a long way down, but we held our collective breaths as he jumped. He ended up with a badly sprained ankle.

Eventually, Gary grew up to be a very loving man. He put all of us through our paces first, though. He began to settle down when he met Donna. She was a cheerleader, and our crazy, wild man fell in love. He didn't talk about it much, but we all knew. We were thrilled when they married, and we fell in love with Stephanie Rita, their beautiful little girl. When she was just a few months old, Gary and Donna brought her to California. She was precious and adorable, and Mom and Dad were so glad to spend some time with her too.

Thank goodness for Continental Airlines! We are so close to the three of them to this day because Gary, Donna, and Stephanie have flown out to be with us, as well as our family in Michigan and Atlanta too. Patty never tired of having Gary and Donna take Stephanie to the Bloated Goat (the bar in Fowlerville where Patty worked for several years). Stephanie would sing "Achy Breaky Heart," and Patty said the whole bar would clap and cheer. We are grateful to them. All three of my kids adore their aunt Donna, and they love playing tricks on their uncle Gary! Of course, he always starts it! Some things never change, thankfully.

The beautiful Russian doctor came in and spoke with us regarding Patty's prognosis and how it was decided. That same day she spoke with me alone, and I appreciated her honesty and sensitivity. When I asked her why we couldn't try radiation, she was very candid.

"We can try it, but it won't be for your sister. It will be for all of you."

Patty was too sick, too weak, and the cancer was too advanced. More importantly, the cancer would probably return. She spoke of her mother and a similar experience, and I suddenly felt very close to her. When she first walked into the room, she had seemed almost detached—doctorly, I guess would be my word for it. But I saw genuine caring and concern for Patty and our family. We walked to the chapel together, and she asked if we'd like a visit from the chaplain. I quickly agreed.

Patty seems irritated. Does her head hurt? Is her body aching from the fibromyalgia? Buffy looks weary, so very tired. The chaplain arrives. She is pleasant, but she calls Patty "Patricia." Our parents would call us by our full names mostly when we were in trouble, and I asked her to call her Patty. Somehow it makes us all feel better. She is kind, and her voice is soothing. We need that. She prays with us and for us, and, for a moment, there is peace in the room.

'There is talk of moving Patty to a convalescent home. We are in Ann Arbor; we will be leaving soon for Patty's final destination. I am afraid to leave this huge hospital. Both Mom and Dad live in convalescent-type homes in California. We have been blessed out here to have two of the best possible homes for Mom and Dad, but not all are like those two. I am afraid because I know, for Patty, they will not help prolong her life; we know they will monitor and watch as her life slips away. There were some problems that have now been worked out, so we are preparing to leave Ann Arbor. The sky is so gray this Thursday morning. The whole world, or at least this part, understands that a blue, beautiful sky would be inappropriate right now. St. Joseph's Hospital in Ann Arbor has been kind and compassionate to us. We'll not forget their kindness.

Buffy is driving her van, and Jackie, Gary, and I are following in our rented jeep. This day it is raining, and it is around 50 degrees, typical late November weather. We follow Buffy into

Howell to the Medilodge Convalescent Home. It is a dark and dreary day. Patty is already there; they are getting her settled in. There will be no more IVs for her. This frightens us because she's had no food for five days and only a few sips of water. How will she live? I go in with Buffy to complete the necessary paperwork, and soon Roger joins us. We are given pamphlets from the palliative care nurse that detail the art of dying or what we can expect from here on out. I am already sick of the word process. I think of processing foods and processing paperwork, but it just doesn't fit in here. Euphemisms-screw them.

Surely this lady understands that we are all adjusting to this death sentence when just a week ago we were trying to decide if Meniere's disease and fibromyalgia would continue adversely affecting Patty in so many chronically bad ways. Meniere's disease (a problem in the inner ear that causes fluid buildup, resulting in a myriad of problems, such as nausea and vertigo) was horrible for Patty for a few years, but it wasn't something we feared would end her life, although it certainly altered it.

The nurse speaks passively and passionately at the same time. She has helped many families as their loved ones made their "transition" (another word we will grow to hate), and there are some common threads. We are reminded of what will be coming in terms that we can understand. I can't speak for Buffy, but after the first few sentences, I tuned her out. I am not ready. Furthermore, if God wants to, he could heal her, this second, the next, or the next. I am not ready.

That first day we were at Medilodge, we saw Tina, Buffy's very close friend. We knew her from Buffy's childhood and Buffy's wedding, but we would come to know her on a whole different level. She is beautiful on the outside but even more beautiful on the inside. She shared a wonderfully unique relationship with Patty, and this news hit her hard too. Patty has been like a second mother to Tina; her heart is in turmoil too. The hospice people have suggested music and massage therapy for Patty. She suffers from fibromyalgia, though, so the therapy is out.

Several weeks earlier, I had bought an Indian spiritual music tape. I had tossed it into my suitcase, and now I brought it out. If it didn't help, it couldn't hurt. Perhaps music could soothe Patty's soul and ours. Patty's demeanor has changed in the last day or so. She had been quiet and occasionally uttered a few words, but she'd become restless and disturbed. Geez, I wonder why! She'd been going through those stupid (now they seemed stupid-not at the time) tests for years; she felt terrible all the time and missed work because she couldn't even stand up due to the Meniere's or perhaps, as we now know, the brain cancer. And now, this!

Patty hadn't eaten anything for days, but there was this sweet nurse who looked at us and asked, "What's her favorite food? Maybe we could entice her to eat."

We were literally begging her to take a few sips of water periodically. They told us later that was probably a good thing, which only served to make us sadder. The nurses were insinuating that the more fluids or foods she ate, the harder Patty's struggle would become at the end. Saturday, Connie will be here. It became something of a mantra for me. It is unbelievably frustrating to see someone in so much obvious pain and not be able to do anything but watch. It was agonizing for her and for us. There is anger and frustration from Patty.

I'm sorry, my sweet sister, but we cannot take the pain away; we cannot even lessen it. I am sorry you have struggled so hard for so very long. *More agitation drugs, please!*

It's a long night. We all stay—Jackie, Buffy, Tina, Loretta, and me. I continue to be grateful that Buffy has Roger. He has maintained his rock-solid status. Loretta is incredible, also. She is suffering so terribly, yet she moves around the room, trying to help everyone any way she can. She lived very close to Patty, and she spent a great deal of time with her. My sweet Brad (Patty's son) is here now. Even though he's at least thirty, I want to hug him and tell him everything will be all right, but that's a lie. Everything in his life will never be the same again. Brad, who married Nikki, a young woman with natural beauty and an amazing smile, will be a changed young man. Jackie and I met their two sons that afternoon. Tyler is five and Jorden is three, and we fell completely in love with them both. They are sweet, polite, and boys! Jorden looks exactly like Brad, and I have the sweetest flashbacks when I see him. I wonder, as I sit beside them both, how I will be able to leave them, not knowing when I will play/talk/hold/love them again.

It seems everyone in this place either knows Buffy or Patty or they simply have compassion for us and want to help. We are deeply moved as moment after moment more help and support arrives from someone in this place. We are fortunate, all things considered. There is an extra bed in Patty's room, and they've told us they will leave it empty so that we can rest if we can. This night has been extremely difficult for Patty. We are asking for the chaplain.

One thing in particular I remember is a time when Patty and I slept downstairs in a closet by the dining room for a little while. I don't remember why Mom put us in there, but it was a tiny little closet with room only for a small bed. The bedspread on that little bed had those strings at the bottom. Every night, Patty and I would pull a few of those strings and play Cat's Cradle until late in the night. So every night, the bedspread would become more and more naked. I don't remember if I won or if one of us won; in fact, I don't even know how to tell if you won. But I do remember how angry Mom was when she found that naked bedspread. We didn't get to sleep in the closet anymore. While we did have a few games that we could play, like Twister, Monopoly, and Aggravation, mostly we played sports outside. We were so lucky to have neighbors with big families on both sides of us. We had two whole teams of whatever sport we played, all the time!

We ask the nurses if they can up Patty's medication. She is very upset almost all of the time. Music doesn't seem to help. It's much more difficult for her to rest. By this time people have heard that Patty is here, and friends and acquaintances are stopping by. We grew up in Fowlerville, which is a town about seven miles from Howell. Many people from Fowlerville work in Howell, and Buffy actually has worked here at Medilodge in the past. Patty works in Howell also. She tends the bar and waitresses at a place called Wranglers. Patty's boss, Angela, is here, and she's trying to help us too. I have known about her through Patty for two years, and I already like her. She is a true friend in every sense of the word. She is one of us now.

We meet Barb. Barb is Patty's RN, and we appreciate her matter-of-fact approach. We may not like what she tells us, but we need honesty. She says they can't up the pain dosage because it could kill her. Oh, the irony. We understand, though, and we draw closer and closer to her. She feels our pain. She's learned a bit of Patty's story, and she feels connected to her now. We can talk to Barb about anything, anytime. And Jamie. Jamie makes us laugh and smile, even when we think we can't. From the nurses, to the aides, to the office personnel, to food servers, to custodians, we are on the receiving end of so much assistance. It has not gone unnoticed by any of us.

Patty is strong. She has had no food or water for days, yet her body hasn't weakened. She wants off the bed now! She gets angry when soothing voices remind her that she must stay in bed. They've brought in a special bed for her fibromyalgia that inflates/deflates periodically, and we are hopeful it will provide some measure of comfort. It may help her body, but it doesn't do much for her mood. This, we will learn, is a part of the transition process also. I want her to have peace. Dear God, please let Patty have peace. This poor little thing could never catch a break. Can she please at least die peacefully, please, God?

I remember the hematite necklace I'm wearing. It will bring peace to her, I feel sure. I take it off. Slowly, I carefully raise her head and slide it over and down her neck, onto her chest. I breathe a sigh of relief that I have finally found a way to help her. It's not on her chest thirty seconds before she reaches for it, tugging and pulling at it, generally letting me know she wants it off right now! I take it off and lay it gently on the pillow beside her. I worry it cannot work if it is not touching her body, but I don't want to aggravate her any more than she is already. There are two chaplains here. One has come in and sat with us. He sang "The Garden" to Patty and spoke warmly and gently to her. She is calm. We are grateful.

More friends drop in. Many are shocked. One said, "She just waited on me last week! "Several shared stories about Patty and how she helped them, even when she was very sick herself. Many stories of selflessness, love for others, and a desire to help. We all share a common bond, and none of us is prepared to lose this beautiful woman.

# JayJay

JayJay (Hayseed) has flown in. We haven't seen him in eight years. He came to Buffy's wedding, and then he dropped out of sight. That was pretty common for him. I understand JayJay. We have always been close. He and I were close as kids, and we continue to be close as adults. I'd spoken with JayJay in October, and he was leaving for Boise, Idaho. He told me then he would get in touch when he was settled in, and I hadn't heard from him since. I got the call from Connie on November 28th, so quite a bit of time had passed without anyone hearing from him. As soon as we all heard about Patty, we started calling JayJay, but to no avail. Eventually, we stopped calling him. Ironically, as Jackie and I landed in Detroit, my cell phone went off. It was Jay Jay. I grabbed the phone, yelling, "Don't hang up! Don't hang up! "He calmly told me he'd already gotten the word and he was coming home. Relief. Jayjay knew and he was coming.

Jayjay and I share very similar personalities. I know Jayjay has struggled with so many demons (we all have), and I felt very sorry for him. He was the first boy, and even though he was young, he felt compelled to protect Mom from Dad. While we used to envy him because he got a new bicycle and a motorcycle, he paid for it in other ways. He could never measure up in Dad's eyes, and not having that really hurt JayJay. To this day, he tells stories of accomplishments turned into disappointments by Dad. There is something inherently wrong with parents who choose to remind their children of their shortcomings, never their successes. It makes it almost impossible to try to achieve goals for yourself or even to set goals for yourself. That negativity manifests itself in such a way inside your brain that first you must overcome your own inability to believe in you.

JayJay was two when Dad first started hitting Mom. He gave her concussions, pulled the phone off the wall, and scared the hell out of us. It scared JayJay so much, but as he got older, he always got involved. Waiting. Listening. Was he going for the gun? We couldn't call the police. We'd always see Dad's angry face screaming and spitting. We were grabbing Mom, screaming that she must leave; he was going for the gun. We all left the house; some of us grabbed the two youngest boys because they were very little. We wondered each time who would die. Would he shoot Mom? Would he kill anyone that's close to her?

Jayjay, as he grew older took a more active role in trying to end the fights. He got angrier and angrier at Dad. Once, when I was about eleven, we ran outside with Mom, and she went with everyone else in the other direction, and I was standing in the road, about 100 feet away. Suddenly, I heard JayJay's voice screaming at me. I looked and saw my dad on the porch with a gun, and he was pointing it at me!

"Hit the ditch! "JayJay yelled.

I did. There was no shot. JayJay lowered the gun and attempted to take it away from Dad. I crawled on my belly up to the neighbor's house (about 200 yards). I wondered if I died. Did I get shot, and I just didn't know it yet? I knew he was pointing the gun at me. I also knew he was a good shot. He had killed many a pheasant, squirrel, rabbit, and deer. He could kill me too. I stood up at the neighbors' and looked for blood. There wasn't any, but I was filthy. I was frightened as I knocked on the door to wake the neighbors. The fights with my parents seemed to never happen during the day, always late at night. The wife opened the door, and I told her the story. She hugged me, laid me down on the couch, and said to go to sleep; she'd take care of everything. I did. I ran home as soon as I woke up, and things were back to normal, or our version of normal: complete and utter chaos.

I thanked JayJay for saving my life. My siblings were angry with me because they said our neighbor never called the police, and they'd stayed outside long into the night. I felt badly; I'd gotten some sleep.

JayJay was diagnosed with an ulcer when he was five. The doctor told Mom he'd never seen that before. JayJay internalized so much of what happened to us that it was no wonder. JayJay wrote wonderful poetry, but he didn't keep it. He and I would often try to see who could come up with the biggest words in our conversations. We always wanted to see which of us had the greater vocabulary. Most people didn't understand it, but we had a lot of fun doing it, and it was a great diversion. JayJay taught me how to shoot a gun-or should I say, he attempted to.

I will never forget the first time he took me out hunting. It was a brisk fall day, and we had JayJay's 4-10 gun with us. We walked into the woods and carefully perched atop a fallen tree trunk. JayJay pointed at the top of a tree; he showed me how to hold the gun, putting the bead through the sights steadily, patiently. There was a bird on the branch as I lined the bead up with the sights, carefully resting the butt of the gun against my chest and holding the barrel with my left hand. I lowered the gun. I didn't want to kill that little bird, and we were both relieved when it flew away a few seconds later. We walked aimlessly for a while, neither of us saying much—I learned quickly that talking doesn't mix well with hunting-until we saw it. It was a great big bull! It didn't seem to be enclosed at all, and he was staring right at us. JayJay was calm; I wanted desperately to scream and run for my life. JayJay had us walk backward, slowly, until we were out of the bull's vision, and then we ran fast!

As we were walking home, we saw some rabbits a short distance away. Jayjay handed me the gun again, and I lined one of the rabbits into my sights. Once again, I couldn't bring myself to do it. I lowered the gun, and I thought I was going to cry. He was very understanding, and he told me not to worry about it. I'd also wasted an opportunity for JayJay to kill a rabbit, though, and I felt even worse about that. The animals killed were always dressed out and eaten, and that could have been a meal. He didn't mention it anymore. He knew I'd tried, but I just wasn't a hunter.

JayJay was about twelve and I was about fifteen when we decided to take matters into our own hands-sort of. We'd become very tired and weary of Dad's raging episodes, and we sat together to try to think of a way to stop it. Even though we knew we'd get a beating if Dad found out, we decided to do it anyway. First, we gathered up all of Dad's shotguns and rifles (there were quite a few). Unfortunately, in order for our plan to work, we needed to take the boys' guns too. We pulled the incinerator away from its resting spot and began to dig. And dig. Finally, we had a huge hole, and we dropped all the guns into it. We quickly covered the hole up and dragged the incinerator back where it was. We worked fast, and when we were finished, we hugged each other. We knew Dad could use other things as weapons; however, we knew we'd removed his most accessible.

Dad never mentioned it; in fact, shortly after that, Dad stopped hitting Mom. He always said it was because he'd gone to a doctor who'd prescribed some little white pills that helped him control his temper. We all knew it was because Mom had started telling him every night that he should sleep with one eye open and that she had had enough.

JayJay went into the army after high school. He was stationed in Korea, and I know it was a good experience for him. While there wasn't a war going on over there, it still troubled us back at home. When he came home, he became a bit elusive. I think all the time he was over there, coupled with all the ugly stuff we'd lived through, probably made him believe he was better off at a distance. No one could blame him for that. Jayjay walks in and out of our lives, but we are so glad that he is in right now.

It is good to see JayJay. He looks well but tired. He walks to Patty's bed, takes her hand, and speaks softly to her. She lets him know she knows he is here. She speaks with her eyes now, but her words are clear. There are six of us here now; we are praying fervently that Connie and Darryl get here before...

The chaplain has been in several times. Friday night becomes increasingly difficult. Patty is restless; the pain is relentless. All of the hearts in this room are heavy and burdened. Desperation. Everyone makes a circle in her room, and we all pray silently and aloud for God to ease her misery. Linda and Rich, Gary, Buffy, Jackie, Loretta, Tina, JayJay, and I gather together, sobbing. praying. Please, we beg you, God, please don't make her suffer any longer. Dear God, can you hear us? Do you hear us? Help her and help us, please!

Gary, Jackie, and Jayjay leave. Gary and Jayjay are staying in a hotel close by, and Jackie is staying at Buffy's, watching the kids. Gary's foot is beginning to swell because he's been on it too much, and he needs to get off it for a while. Donna, Gary's wife, is here now with Stephanie, and I am so glad to see her. Donna is a true sister (not by law, by love). Many years ago, Donna gave me a plaque with words about how we'd become sisters by chance and friends by love. It was so very true. She fits in everywhere in our family, and we all love her. Donna has lost several loved ones, some very recently, and we look to her for guidance and advice. We need to also remember, though, that Donna will struggle as we are because she's very close to Patty too.

Stephanie is having a difficult time. She loves her aunt very much. While they are in the room, our nurse, Barb, comes in. We have been watching Patty struggle to take one of her pills that she desperately needs. It goes under her tongue, and it's supposed to dissolve, but Patty has no saliva left, and it just sits there. Barb tells us she will crush it and put it in something for her. She brings back some kind of pudding or gelatin, but it dissolves in Patty's mouth. Thank God! We are relieved, and most of us just want to hug Barb for getting us through this incredibly difficult moment.

We are coming and going in shifts now. We are occupying

the nurses lounge and the visitors' room, as well as a spare room they've provided us. Patty's friends continue to stream in. The looks are all the same: disbelief, sadness, hurt, and always a desire to help us in any possible way. Patty hasn't had any fluids for many days, and she's had no food for over a week now. Still, her spirit is unbroken.

They have hooked her up to oxygen. The hospice ladies come; the medication is increased. The ladies take her vital signs and tell us Patty may not make it through the weekend. While you can know things sometimes, really know things, when they are spoken aloud, it's as if we are hearing it for the first time. We are all shocked to hear that statement. Buffy is devastated. She reminds me that just a week ago Patty was at her house, preparing for radiation. She was certainly not well, but she was walking and talking-living.

It is difficult to comprehend this moment-by-moment reality. We are waiting, staring at Patty. She is peaceful only briefly now, with hard moments much of the time. When Patty cries out and sits up, we all try to comfort her. It is to no avail. She wants out of bed, and she seems to have the strength of Popeye. I try to convince her to go someplace in her mind where she can find peace. I ask her to try to see the ocean. Her favorite place in California has always been Newport Beach. Every time she'd visit, I'd want to take her somewhere she'd never been, but that was where she always wanted to go; it became something of a sanctuary for her. For a while, Patty transports herself to the beach.

"Can you see the water, Patty? Can you smell the ocean? Can you see the beautiful birds?"

She nods her head. She almost smiles. She has relaxed a bit, which is some measure of comfort for everyone, however short-lived. Calm, for this moment, has been restored.

*Patty at one of her favorite place – Newport Beach*

Night has turned into day. Patty has struggled but lived through this night. Hollow, trance-like eyes everywhere. Vacant, lost looks. I still remain hopeful. God can do anything. He could save her this moment or the next. Today is Saturday. Connie comes today.

# Connie

The third daughter, Connie (Condor), is the one who should have been a model. She is tall, beautiful, confident, and self-assured.

Connie lives in Atlanta and has her own business. She knows how to handle every situation. This one will be the exception, however. She is incredibly close to Patty, and I know this will crush her heart. Her tough exterior belies her gentle nature inside.

Connie never cared about who was mad at her or didn't like her. If she felt she was in the right, she would not back down-ever.

Case in point: Dad would always make us cut our own switch (punishing rod, usually part of a tree branch or plant) so he could whip us with it. There was a time when Connie got into big trouble. I do not know what she did, but Dad was angry with her. He told her to cut him a switch. She walked outside and told us she wasn't going to do it. Then she took off into the woods. Dad was furious! He yelled for us to go tell her if she didn't come back she was going to get it even worse. We ran down the lane leading into the woods, and we pleaded with her to come home so she wouldn't get beat even worse, but she refused. We were so worried. We knew she was really going to get it. Well, she sat in a tree for hours, and, by the time she came home, Dad had fallen asleep. She wasn't punished at all!

One of the times when Dad chased Mom out of the house, we snuck her back in through the backdoor. Connie stood at the door as a decoy, but Dad figured out what we were up to. He started in the door, but Connie pushed him out and locked the door. Dad took his fist and put it through the glass and into Connie's face. Fortunately, she wasn't scarred, but he could have killed her.

Connie lost her voice when she was young. Mom took her to several doctors and specialists, but no one could diagnose the problem. It lasted for about a year. Mom, who had injured her back at the factory where she worked, had been on disability. After a while, the factory decided to settle with her. The day Mom got her disability check, Connie spoke her first words in a year. "Mama's a rich woman! We were all so happy she got her voice back-for a while anyway. You knew I had to say that, Connie!

Connie went to school at Michigan State University. I will always remember one year when I picked her up for the summer, and she had a friend with her—and a dog! I freaked out because it was a big dog, a boxer. Connie said she'd been the mascot and no one else would take her. On the way home, that dog put her face on the back of my seat and very close to my neck. I kept imagining she was going to bite me and that I would die because Connie wanted to save a dog. Well, she grew on me. We all fell in love with Gator, but she really became my dog. She was faithful, devoted, and loving.

I grew up envious of Connie's beauty and popularity. I wanted to hang around with her and go to parties with her too, but for some reason, she didn't want me to. Connie is the family rock. Her pragmatic manner would be necessary as we edged closer and closer.

Linda and Rich picked Connie up in Flint. As difficult as I know it has been for her, Connie has begun piecing together an obituary. She was working on it as she prepared to come back to Michigan. We are all grateful; none of us had even started thinking about that. She has also brought some CDs. Hopefully they will provide some solace as well. We are alternating between my Indian spiritual music and Alan Jackson's treasured hymns. Every one of those songs is beautiful, and we know them all, but I can hardly bear hearing the words, "Softly and tenderly,

Jesus is calling/calling for you and for me/calling, "Oh sinner, come home."

Connie is surprised at how much Patty has deteriorated in the few days since she had seen her. Patty's hair is turning all gray; it seems to be changing by the minute. I cannot begin to tell you how much it hurt to hear a nurse talking to me about Patty, referring to her as "your mother." The battle inside Patty rages on; she is weakened, the cancer rapidly consuming her body, yet she fights. What a struggle it must be inside her right now with reconciling death and desperately wishing to live at the exact same time. This wonderful mother and grandmother would never choose to leave them—never. They are her life. It is her absolute existence.

The humming/swooshing of the oxygen machine in the room is the only thing I can hear right now. It continues in a relentless pattern, struggling to keep Patty alive as the cancer fights more aggressively to take it. How long, I wonder, will that machine stay in here with us? The palliative care women have spoken with us. Patty languishes, albeit with more medication given even more frequently now. The two women tell us something that had not occurred to us. They say that Patty may be hanging on because she wants to "transition" alone. We are stunned. The lady tells us that sometimes people would rather not have their loved ones around them, and she cites some examples as well. Could Patty be one of them? While Patty was oftentimes a very private person, it seemed unfathomable that she'd prefer not having us there.

Emotions are raging out of control for most of us. Connie, who is known for being straightforward. reminds us that maybe the hospice people are correct. She also lets Buffy and me know that some of the rest of the family are upset because they want to be alone with Patty too. I am hurt. I haven't really left Patty for any length of time since I have been here. We arrived on Tuesday evening; today is Saturday.

While I probably would have done the same thing anyway, I

am feeling badly because I was kind of angry with Patty before all this happened. It seems silly now, of course, but a few months earlier, Patty, Linda, Rich, Loretta, Roger, Buffy, Brad, Nikki, and their children all went to Atlanta to see Connie. Everyone was there except for Jackie and me. Patty and I talked before they left, and she said they would call me from Atlanta so I could talk to everyone. No one called me. I learned later that both Patty and Linda weren't well down there, but, at the time, I was awfully hurt, especially when Dad called me on one of those days to say—in his own boastful way—that he'd spoken with Connie and she told him everything they were doing down there. So the last time I spoke with Patty was before they left for Atlanta. I call her often, but she was so sick with her vertigo from the Meniere's most of the time she really couldn't call me back. At any rate, I felt guilty and sad about that, but mostly, I just wanted to be with her every minute.

So, Buffy and I left, and we went to her house. I got to spend some time with Jacob, Buffy, and Roger's eighteen-month-old son, who is just adorable and busy, busy, busy. Branden—I hadn't seen him since Buffy's wedding when he was three, and now he's twelve—and Brad's two sons, Tyler and Jorden. Roger put up a tent in the living room, and Jacob, Tyler, Jorden, and I sang, ran around, and laughed together. It was just what I needed.

Branden was at school, but we spent time later together cooking and baking. We made Mexican food and cornbread, but we made a memory together that we'll cherish forever. He is such a polite young man, and he is absolutely charming. I watched little Jacob in the living room trying to do somersaults with the other boys, and my heart hurt. He will never know his grandma the way he should. I hope with all my heart that Jorden and Tyler remember Patty. I know Branden has his own very special, loving memories of his grandmother.

*Grandma Patty with Jacob, Buffy and Roger's little boy.*

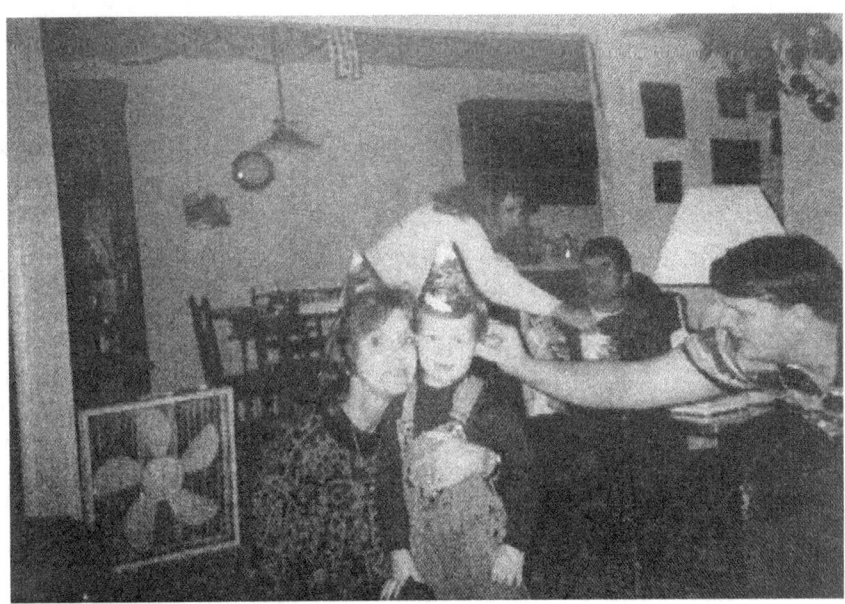

*Grandma Patty with Branden, Roger and Buffy's older boy.*

*Grandma Patty with Tyler, Brad and Nikki's older boy.*

*Grandma Patty with Jorden, Brad and Nikki's younger boy.*

Later, Buffy and I went through Patty's picture albums and her music. We put several pictures and CDs aside for later. We stayed away from the convalescent home for most of the morning and part of the afternoon. Patty has been left alone for some time throughout the day, yet she hasn't left us. We decide she isn't one of those individuals who prefer to be alone when they transition.

Brother David is here now too. David grew up down the road from us, and he is like a brother to us all. He belongs here. Connie babysat for David when he was young, and his parents were very kind to her, as well as the rest of us. He lives just a few minutes from Medilodge, and we are glad to see him. Julie, his sweet wife, is with him, and she is a blessing to us. She has traversed this path before; she knows what we are experiencing.

Patty's friends and coworkers trickle in and out with disbelief etched on their faces. We have become accustomed to phrases such as "I just saw her!" and "How could this happen so fast?"

Aunt Jeanette, Mom's sister; her friend, Charlie; Uncle Jimmy, Mom's deaf brother; and his wife, Helen, who is also deaf, arrive. They live in Flint, where Linda and Rich live, which is about an hour's drive from Medilodge. It is so good to see Aunt Jeanette. I wish she could make it all go away like she used to when we were little. Aunt Jeanette and her husband, Uncle Ang, had three children of their own, but they always made us feel very special and loved.

Sadly, a few years ago, Uncle Ang passed away. He was just one of the nicest men God ever placed on this earth. He was kind, gentle, yet fun-loving too. We are all wondering if Uncle Ang is here with us right now, helping Patty as she hovers between life and not-life. We all hope and pray that he is. Being there with them in those years was a different, therapeutic world for us. This time, however, they won't be able to take the pain away. This time they will feel it too.

Aunt Jeanette, Uncle Jimmy, and his wife go in to see Patty.

When they come out, Aunt Jeanette struggles to compose herself and says, "I can't believe it. She's always been so feisty!"

We all sit in silence for a while. There are just no words. Buffy is exhausted, and Brad's face reveals deep, painful heartache. The two had become accustomed to hearing Patty was sick. Problems with her fibromyalgia and Meniere's disease kept her in doctors' offices and ER rooms more than they could count, but how had this time become so final?

Brad is trying to be brave, but it is so tough. Roger is here often, and he speaks to Patty with love and respect. He calls her "Mom," and I know he means it; he genuinely loves her like a mother. Roger, the rock, is beginning to show signs of the strain. He is still trying to work, even though it's the night shift, and he's also trying to take care of the kids during the day. Jackie has been staying there at night to watch the boys so Buffy can stay with Patty. It is probably more difficult there for her, waiting, not knowing. Roger and Buffy are grateful to her because they know the boys are in good hands. Our days and nights are all blending in. We know it is Sunday. Darryl comes today.

# Darryl

Darryl Lee (Toad, Toadstool, Dodo, Dodie, Butterball—that one given to him by our aunts) is the baby of the family. He was a roly-poly little guy with the cutest blond curls and a good disposition. He just seemed to roll with things. He never, ever got in a hurry, though, and trying to make him rush was a waste of time and energy. Darryl always smiled and seemed never to have a harsh word for anyone. How did he get into this family?

Darryl was a good boy who was also very quiet. I'm not sure if it was his nature or if he just got tired of opening his mouth and having Gary shove something into it. We'd get so mad at him because he'd stay in the bathroom for hours taking his bath, and when he came out, only his arms were clean. You could actually see the line where clean stopped and filth began. When pressed, he admitted to floating his boats in the tub and forgetting to climb in with them. He started really bathing when girls came into the picture, though.

Darryl and his friend David were inseparable. They would spend every possible moment they could together. They played cars and trucks, made mud pies (messes), cut out big cucumbers from our garden to make canoes, and they listened to Johnny Cash over and over again.

Darryl is here with us now. We are together, all eight of us. Has Patty been holding on until Darryl got here? If so, she can go now. Darryl sits by Patty, holding her hand stoically. He is still our baby brother, and we wonder how he will handle this.

But Darryl believes in a spiritual transition, and that will help him. Some moments I feel that way too, but they are fleeting. I still don't get why this has to happen. She needs to stay here for her kids, grandchildren, nieces and nephews, friends, and us.

Patty no longer tries to sit up. She doesn't yell out that she needs to pee. The hospice nurses explain, in graphic detail, where we are in terms of the end of Patty's journey. Patty is trying to come to terms with the fact that she is dying. She never had time to fully grasp her diagnosis.

Before she lapsed into the coma, she believed she'd be starting radiation for her brain cancer. She is trapped between these two worlds: the living and the not. She continues to hear us, though. We know because she still acknowledges us with her eyes. She knows... For a while now, we've seen Patty completely lost in some kind of conversation with someone not in this room. She smiles, moves her lips as if speaking to someone, and we know. We still hope she's communicating with Uncle Ang and maybe our two grandmothers. They are here, we pray, to stay with her and help her when her spirit leaves, and we cannot.

We have a formidable task ahead of us. Patty continues in this state, we believe, because she knows how much we all need her here. Yet we know that without divine intervention, she will die. We must allow her to go by letting her know that it's okay, that we will be all right, which, of course, is a complete lie. The challenge before us is to do it convincingly. While it is increasingly difficult for us, hearing Buffy tell Patty that she and Brad will be okay tears at our hearts. Buffy sits on the floor, holding Patty's hand, and she talks to Patty about the strength she has because of her. Patty is aware of everything she is saying. She nods/smiles/blinks, letting her little girl know she hears her. We are so proud of Buffy. She is lying to her mother better than she ever has before, and Patty believes her. She must.

Brad too must let Patty know that he will be all right. He has tremendous inner strength, and he is clearly drawing on everything he has. Patty can only have a peaceful transition if she knows the two reasons her heart has continued to beat this long will get through.

Both of them share stories with Patty. We can hardly believe this is the same Patty from a few minutes ago! She smiles often as they tell funny stories and sweet, personal times for them. She is with only the two of them for these moments, and it is gratifying to see. It's a world only the three of them know. It is fitting that she, even briefly, shows them that love will conquer pain every time. It's almost as if she was her old self, and we relish this God-given moment. Brad and Buffy do for our sister what only they can do: light up her face, light up her life. It is gone so quickly, but it changes everything.

The next morning, the nurse checks Patty, saying, "Her feet are beginning to mottle."

*Mottle* sounds like "model" to me, and I do not like this word at all. I do not know what to feel at this moment; there is an overwhelming sadness passing through my entire body. Ending is near. Lifeless feet. Oh God, no. Hurry, God, please hurry. Don't let this happen. We are torn. This, we know, must happen. And even though it's scary, frightening, and alarming, somewhere way down inside us, we feel a tiny sense of relief. Many of us can only stay a few more days, and we would hate to leave knowing Brad and Buffy would be here alone. Our hearts are twisted. We don't know how to feel or think anymore. I just stare. There is a growing ache in my heart.

Someone asks, "Should we call Mom and Dad?"

# Mom

Where to start? I always say the word cantankerous did not exist until our Dad. Since my siblings and I never really got to see Dad interact with his family (he and Mom moved to Michigan from West Virginia after Connie was born), we don't know what kind of brother or son he was. We do know, however, what kind of husband and father he was. Mom's stories about Dad in his younger days are what I use to complete his picture. She shared the story of their first date. It was fitting-for them. Mom said that as they stood together outside in front of her house that first night, a mouse ran up Dad's leg. It startled him so much he dropped his pants! The mouse scurried back down his leg, and it took off running, probably scaring the mouse more than Dad. That probably should have told Mom a little something about Dad's appeal to the rodent family.

Mom married Dad when she was sixteen; he was twenty-one. She told us that she wanted to marry Dad even though she was too young. You had to be twenty-one in those days, even in West Virginia. Mom was determined, however, and they proceeded to get married. Mom said that when the preacher asked if she was over twenty-one, she said yes. And she wasn't lying; she was over twenty-one; her grandfather had put twenty-one cents in her shoe so it wouldn't be a lie. We were straight-up hillbillies. Now I am proud of that, but in those years in Michigan, we felt embarrassed. All of us kids tried hard to get rid of that drawl. A simple "hi" became "hiiii," and "all of you" became Y'all." Mom and Dad haven't stopped drawling, even though they lived in Michigan for many years and California for twenty years. I realize now that it kind of defines them, and I think they want to hang on to that part of themselves.

I know life wasn't easy for them, having children so rapidly with little or no money. Mom was either extremely talented or incredibly good at adapting to any situation. Mom sewed all of us girls' clothes until Jackie was five; that's a long time. After the boys were born, she went to work at a factory. She and Dad both worked nights, and until Linda could take care of us, Mrs. Royce would come and stay with us. She had older sons, so she could stay with us throughout the night. We loved her. She'd stand at the bottom of the stairs, and in a voice just loud enough for all eight of us to hear, she would read the Bible. It was quiet and mellow.

Mrs. Royce brought peace and tranquility into our very strange, chaotic lives. Perhaps everyone has parts of their lives where anger and fear live, but they only show the sedate, perfect side. We were always one extreme or the other, such as going to church on Sunday morning and being frightened to death that Dad would kill Mom that night. In those years, we would ask ourselves, "What on earth could Mom do or have done that is so bad Dad feels justified in killing her?"

There were so many difficulties involved with us as young people. Trying to learn at school was unbelievably tough as we struggled with the everyday problems at home. Our parents presented a very different picture in front of other people. In fact, many people who knew Dad well refused to believe he was capable of giving Mom concussions and pulling out guns. It was disturbing to us because he had a Jekyll/Hyde personality, and we knew both of them all too well, unfortunately.

Mom struggled with back problems much of her married life. She got hurt at the factory where she worked. It began with a herniated disc in her lumbar area. Mom would spend several months out of every year in the hospital, and one of us girls would always ride in the ambulance. Dad refused to go-ever. We were young, maybe twelve or thirteen, when we'd go with her. We lived about fifteen miles from the nearest hospital, and in the winter the weather was always treacherous, which made that trip so much longer. Mom would be screaming and crying in agony. It was so hard to sit next to her and see it and not be able to help her in any way. Much of mom's life was spent in the hospital, in traction, in pain.

Mom didn't drink or smoke until all of her kids were born; she was twenty-nine. Dad, on the other hand, started smoking in his early teens. He smoked for over fifty years until he had the stroke five years ago. Dad also drank moonshine at an early age.

Mom began drinking heavily when her back problems worsened. The factory gave Mom a monetary settlement, but it did little to lessen her pain. She went back to work, though. Mom would always tell us how she made plastic things for hospitals, like emesis basins. Even when she was in the hospital, she'd remark that she could have made that very basin. Of course we shared that exciting information with all of our friends. Our friends all loved Mom. Many of them called her "mom" also.

Mom often had two or three jobs at one time. For a while she sold Sarah Coventry jewelry. I used to love watching Mom carefully open the jewelry-filled box, pull out the cloth-wrapped brooches or earrings, and gingerly unwrap the biggest, gaudiest pieces of jewelry I'd ever seen. She was innovative, and she was always thinking of what she could do next. We were all amazed when Mom began making candles with pictures in the wax. It was really something special if you received one of those gifts from her. She would find pictures of various stages of a child or occasion and embed them into the candle. The final touch would be to drip wax perfectly around those photos, giving the appearance those pictures were a part of the candle as it was being created. It was very unique, very creative, very much Mom.

Mom tried hard to create some fun for us in different ways. She made the best fudge in the world. She never used a recipe. She would make a big batch and dump in some peanut butter after it boiled. She would stir and pour it into butter-covered plates. We would watch her put the fudge into the freezer, knowing it wasn't going to harden, and then we would wait. After a while, she'd pull the plates out of the freezer, and we'd grab spoons. The best fudge in the world is the best fudge because you never measure the ingredients and you always eat it with a spoon-right from the plate.

Snow ice cream! Sounds yummy, right? Well, it actually is. Mom would always let us take pans outside when the snow had just fallen and fill them full. She'd add cream, sugar, and other good stuff, and we had delicious ice cream for a treat at a fraction of the cost of regular ice cream. That, in essence, was Mom. She was always finding ways to use whatever she had available for something.

Mom would make us take a tablespoon of cod liver oil every night. It was gross and disgusting, and we always balked at taking it. Mom would remind us that if we spit it out, we'd get two tablespoons. Patty pushed to see if Mom really meant that, and she did. The problem wasn't so much taking the oil—it was having that terrible fishy taste in your mouth just as you were going to bed. Perhaps we might have been more amenable to it if Mom had given it first thing in the morning. I believe wholeheartedly, though; that's why most of us have stayed so healthy. She really did us a favor.

I broke my arm when I was in third grade. Patty and I were doing the angel balance on a mattress on the floor when I fell and landed on my right arm. Mom and Dad were at work, so our neighbors made me a sling from a diaper, and they took me to the doctor. He set my arm, and Mom came and took me home. It hurt a lot. Mom made me a bed in the living room, and she brought me SpaghettiOs and put it on the bed. I was hungry, but I was right-handed and I couldn't use my arm. So I tried to eat with my left, but spaghetti sauce and noodles got all over Mom's white sheets. She came back awhile later, and I saw her look at the stained sheets. I just knew she was going to be mad, but she just laughed. Then she said it would probably take some doing, but I'd better start practicing doing things with my left hand. To this day, I can write and do several things with both hands thanks to her.

She also was responsible for making me not quit school in the sixth grade. I had been so fortunate to have the greatest two teachers for all my kindergarten through fifth grade, and I wasn't prepared for someone who clearly didn't like me from day one-and I was soon to find out why. The first thing she did was call roll, and when she said my name, I said, "Present."

She just looked angrily at me, saying, "Do you have a sister, Linda?"

"Yes," I stammered.

"Oh no," she said, shaking her head as if the rest of her life was now ruined because of me.

Later, when I was home, I began to cry when I thought about what had happened with the teacher, and I told Mom I was going to quit school. She pulled me into the chair with her and stroked my head. She suggested I take her something the next day, perhaps an apple, and see if that made a difference. I took her an apple. She smiled, thanked me warmly, and after that, she didn't look at me like she hated me anymore, but she didn't look at me like she liked me either. I was able to at least tolerate the sixth grade with her.

The good thing for Mom was that she had all five girls first. We could clean, cook, do laundry, babysit, and clean diapers. Now that task wasn't great anytime, but cloth diapers, diaper pails, and great big diaper pins didn't help. Actually, Mon did most of the pinning. She must have known after cleaning all those diapers, then seeing those great big diaper pins and the little guy who'd messed those diapers...

Mom, who tried hard to feed us food that was good for us, would occasionally make liver for us. While the rest of us didn't care for it, we ate it simply because we knew we couldn't get up from the table until it was gone. Patty, however, refused to eat it every time. We'd all go in and see her sitting at the table, cold liver in front of her, and we'd try to encourage her to eat it so she could get up. She was determined not to eat it. And Mom was determined that she would. Sometimes we'd still see her sitting there late at night. I think Mom eventually gave up and let her go. Mom's persistence with her was only, I believe, because, of all of us, Patty needed that liver the most. She was the skinniest little thing. She was called the "runt of the litter" with good reason.

Mom tried hard for a long time, but life got the best of her eventually. It was rough on all of us with Mom's back problems, but it became so much worse with the alcohol. She would say and do things that were totally out of character for her. I remember one Christmas when I kept asking Mom if she'd shopped for the boys yet, and she told me every day that she had gifts in her closet for them. One day I decided to go in and get them, and Mom stopped me. She said she had something in there for me too, so I couldn't go in. So, I waited.

On Christmas Eve, I told Mom to bring out the gifts so I could wrap them, and then I discovered, to my shock, there was nothing at all in her closet, except some empty liquor bottles. I didn't know what to do, so I called Patty. She quickly decided we were going to pool our money and go to Meier Thrifty Acres. It was late now, close to three in the afternoon, and they closed at six. We raced around the store, trying to find some things for our brothers, and Patty made me buy some things for me too so the boys wouldn't be suspicious. It was crazy, and everything was picked over, but at least we had a few things for the boys to open. Now, on top of Dad's violent rages, we added Mom's alcoholism.

I think for most if not all of us, in those days, the worst part was the words that Mom used in those years. I say it now because if someone should read this book and recognize that they use hurtful phrases when speaking to their children, maybe this will convince them to stop. Mom had two phrases she used with us. Both were terrible. The first one was "You aren't worth the salt it takes to make your bread." That was sad, of course, because oftentimes we made our own bread, and all you added was a pinch of salt—into a great big bowl of dough. However, the second one, "You're not worth the powder it would take to blow your brains out," really cut us to the core. Unfortunately, those remarks, made in anger and probably not meant, would prove to be the biggest hurdle we'd have to overcome. For some of us, it became impossible.

Years later, when my boyfriend was loading his own bullets, he showed me a tiny amount of gunpowder in his hand. He said that's how much went into his bullets. I was speechless! At that moment, all I could think about was how much, or how little, we were thought of. So to whomever reads this book, please remember that the words you choose as you shape and mold your child can make them believe they can do anything, or it can make them believe they can do nothing, that they are less than all other human beings on the face of the earth, and their thoughts, wishes, and beliefs are unimportant to all other people. While we now, as adults, understand why those words were uttered, we will never understand how to forget them. Shortly thereafter, we discovered that things with Mom could and would get much worse.

When Mom first began exhibiting signs of schizophrenia, I think I began to realize how Patty's cool demeanor wasn't just an added bonus but a lifesaving necessity. While our upbringing had been anything but normal, this put a whole different spin on everything. Poor Mom. I think she struggled with it long before it became clear to all of us that she was losing her grip on reality. She was questioning her sense of reality. Had she really seen the angel on her nightstand wink? Was the devil in hot pursuit, even as she carried God's baby inside her? We were all worn out just from our day-to-day existence; we were simply not prepared for this.

Linda was married, and both Ronnie and Loretta were quite

young. Patty was married to Bob. Buffy was about three, and Brad hadn't been born yet. Connie was married, as was Jackie (she was living in Illinois at the time). I had decided, after living life like we had, to skip the marriage and kids. In fact, my mantra was, "If I'm ever stupid enough to get married, I am not going to make it worse by having kids! "Thankfully, for me, God knows what you really want, even if you don't.

I was the only girl still living at home. Fortunately, Patty lived about ten minutes away, and I called her all the time. It was difficult because our three brothers were still young, and we were trying to help them get through too. It was tumultuous, unpredictable and scary. We just never knew, from one moment to the next, when Mom was going to be crazy and when she would be okay. This was Mom? The same person who worked three jobs many times, raised eight kids, had many friends, and was so loved by her brothers and sisters? What was going on?

I was working as a waitress the first time we realized she was delusional and not drunk. I will remember this moment forever because it completely caught me off guard. When I walked in from work, Mom told me to turn off the radio. While I hadn't heard it right away, I went searching for the radio. I looked upstairs, downstairs, and in the basement. No music. Anywhere. I went to the living room where Mom was sitting, and I told her there wasn't any music playing. Then I started looking for a bottle. There wasn't one; she was sober. After telling Mom a second time there was no music playing, she looked at me strangely, asking, "What's happening to me?" I called Patty.

Over the next few weeks, Mom began to separate more and more from reality. *What is the underlying reason?* The whole family wondered. Was it the DTs (delirium tremens)? Not very likely, as she drank excessively, so it wouldn't seem as though she'd be suffering from not having alcohol. Menopause, maybe, but the doctors said this dramatic change would be extremely rare. We were at our wit's end. No one slept in our house. Mom was almost never lucid in those days. She left for ten days and stayed with another man. She wrote a TV preacher a check for a thousand dollars. When I called them and explained that Mom was ill and we needed that money back to make the house payment and buy food for my brothers, they still refused to return the check. I couldn't believe an organization that professes to love all people, care, and give could keep something they knew we desperately needed.

On top of the problems with Mom, money was a bigger problem now. Dad would give me $10.00, and I would buy milk, bread, peanut butter and jelly, and dented cans of soup. Then I would call Patty and cry. Finally, we spoke to our family doctor, and we told him of her driving and not knowing where she was, running through the house with knives in search of the devil, and many other disturbing incidents. He spoke at length with Mom in his office, and then he called us in. He said Mom had become a danger to herself and others, and we should commit her to a psychiatric institution.

After a judge signed the papers, Connie and I drove her to Ann Arbor. We spent hours talking with social workers, nurses, and doctors. Then it was time. We took Mom into the bathroom because the nurses told us Mom had to remove all her jewelry, which proved to be another problem. The bathroom was cold and dark, with no windows and no mirrors. Throughout the day, Mom had been in her own little world. Now, however, she was very aware. She knew, and she was very frightened. So were we. We used soap and pushed and pried to get her rings off. Eventually they slid from her fingers and into our hands. I put them into my purse. Mom began to ask questions.

"Why are we here? Why did you take my jewelry off? When are we leaving? Who are these people?"

We quickly left the bathroom, and the nurse was there, waiting. "No calls for ten days. No visits for two weeks," she said matter-of-factly.

That was the first time we'd heard that, but we tried not to show anything different on our faces. Then we were at the elevator. We hugged Mom, and the nurse firmly guided her into the elevator. Mom was terrified and wild-eyed, unwilling and unable to comprehend what was happening to her.

"Don't leave me here!" She begged. The elevator door closed, yet we could still hear her crying out, "Take me with you, please, please!"

Connie and I got onto the expressway leading us home and away from Mom. We'd made it only a few miles when Connie pulled over, and we both cried and cried. What had we done? Did we do the right thing? She seemed normal at the end—had she suddenly gotten better? We got home, and Patty was there with our three brothers. She assured us that we'd done the right thing. It was the only thing we could have done. She reminded us that we did this to help Mom, something Mom could not understand right now. Mom stayed the first time for about a month. Then she came home, temporarily cured.

For the next several years, she was in and out of that institution. She would seem fine. In fact, she felt so well she believed she didn't need to take her medications. So she wouldn't, and, invariably, she would end up back there for more treatment. I would make the trip twice a week. It was a long, boring trip, and I came to dread it, especially during the times when she didn't recognize me.

When she first went in, she would begin on the first floor, reserved, I believe, for the sickest individuals who seemed to have little or no connection with reality. That was horrible. Patty would go with me as often as she could. Linda had her children and the farm; Connie lived and worked in Lansing, a very long drive from here; and Jackie was still in Illinois. We would get locked in a tiny room with no windows for fifteen minutes. Mom would just sit there, staring in her catatonic way, enclosed in her own world. She'd never respond to anything we said, nor did she look at us. Sometimes, she looked through us. Mostly, she just stared. And we counted the minutes until they unlocked the door. It was unnerving, to say the least. We weren't afraid of our mom, but we weren't always sure about this person sitting in there with us.

After she had taken her meds for a while, they moved her to the second floor, which still wasn't great, but at least she recognized us most of the time. Eventually she'd end up on the third floor; she'd be discharged from this floor when they pronounced her well. Sometimes when Mom was on the third floor, Patty would let me take Buffy with me to visit Mom. It made the trip so much more bearable for me. Buffy was so cute and extremely articulate. She was quite a conversationalist, and she made many friends over there. The doctors and nurses always seemed sad when I went by myself without Buffy; I was too. I almost dreaded the time for her discharge because I knew she would stop taking her medications again and this unfortunate cycle would continue. Finally, she accepted that in order for her to live life to its fullest, she must adhere to something she didn't want to do. She began to take her meds faithfully every day.

Mom and Dad bought the little country store about five miles from our house, and they renamed it "Aunt Myrtle's." They moved into the back part of that store, and our old house went up for sale. Aunt Myrtle's was a success in terms of being something both my parents could do. Finally, Mom was working only one job, although it was a sixteen- to eighteen-hours-a-day job. However, they extended credit to too many people, and they had an even bigger problem: Mom's drinking. We began finding bottles of wine everywhere. Mom was not a pretty drunk. So having beer and wine there at the store proved to be too much of a temptation for Mom. I try not to judge her, though, because I've never had to endure back pain, certainly not the excruciating pain Mom lived with. She suffered, and then she suffered some more. I probably would have drank and taken drugs too. Patty, Connie, and I took Mom to Lansing for a "drying out" weekend. Surprisedly, she stopped drinking. We were proud that she did that and that she didn't start back again.

She had a much more difficult time with smoking; she smoked

until she was seventy-four, even with emphysema and an enlarged heart. But habits like that are hard to break, we know. The doctors told us it is much harder for people with schizophrenia. She tried hypnotism (didn't work), stop-smoking gum (ineffective; she'd smoke and chew that gum at the same time), and patches (didn't work, no matter how many or how strategically placed they were).

It is difficult for all of us to breathe right now because we are feeling so much for Patty. It seems, as each hour passes, that more and more of her body has begun to mottle. No, I do not like that word. Maybe I should say her spirit is moving closer to God. No, I can't. Her breathing is very, very labored now. We hear the phrase "death rattle." Hate that too. Rattles are for babies and snakes. Is she here with us still? Or is she already with Uncle Ang, our grandmas, aunts, and uncles? She does not move, yet she responds when we talk to her, using only her eyes to say the things she knows we need to hear—in any possible form. She is still holding on; that fact continues to amaze us. She's had no food for almost two weeks now and no fluids for several days. We all just touch her, gently kissing her forehead. She's not ready yet. There's something she still must need—or someone.

# Dad

**D**ad. You know a lot about him already, but there is so much more. Only Dad would name our sister Connie after his first wife. Only Dad would beat Mom one night and buy her a huge box of candy the next day. He was good at buying Mom the best gifts. The irony was not lost on us. Hitting, threatening to kill a person, and then showering her with lavish gifts only served to confuse us more.

Dad had his way, however. He would grab Darryl sometimes when he was a few years old and dance to "White Lightning." I don't know if we liked it because it was so cute or if it simply humanized him a bit.

Dad is a sports fanatic. He will watch anything, anytime. He took a few of us to a Detroit Tigers game once, and I was thrilled! We arrived early, and JayJay and I watched Willie Horton warming up. JayJay called out to him, and he turned and waved; I still remember that moment.

Dad could be very loving and giving at times, but those other times stood out so much more. Dad would keep his old razor blades, and every couple of weeks, we'd fight over who got to use them to cut off the corns and calloused skin off his feet. I did mention we didn't have many toys, right? Yes, I fought to do it too, and everyone remembered the last time the other ones had done it. We also scampered around outside with Dad when he'd throw his cigarette butts away. We fought over who got to put those out too. Mom had the most beautiful plants growing when we were kids, and Dad would always put his cigarette butts out in them. When she'd yell at him, he would simply say, "Oh, Myrtle, they're good for plants!"

He had a way about him, though, that women liked. I don't know how many affairs Dad had, but Mom caught him once—big time! Mom had suspected for a long time, and one day she took Jackie—she was probably around ten at the time—to the bar where she thought he'd taken the other woman. Sure enough, they were there. Mom and Jackie peered in through the window outside, and they saw the two of them having drinks at a table.

Jackie watched Mom walk in, go up to Dad's table, call the woman a whore, and she threw Dad's drink in his face. Then she calmly walked out. He probably continued to have affairs, but he was just more discreet. I have always maintained that when people accuse other people of something, as Dad always did to Mom in those years, it's usually because they have something to hide themselves.

To be fair, Mom had some stuff of her own going on also. Dad was a good friend to many of the people in our small town. He developed quite a rapport with neighbors and friends, and we just never quite figured out how we missed out on that. I thought I'd include some of Mom and Dad's favorite phrases and sayings that didn't amuse us as children but now bring a smile to our faces:

"Scriptaphrenia": Dad's way of saying schizophrenia, which always made us think of ink pens.

"Disposition": When Ron and Linda had a court case, they needed Dad to fly from California to Michigan to give his deposition. He kept saying, "I need to give them my disposition!" I kept reminding him that half of Michigan already knew his disposition.

"Frail": Not like fragile, but frail, as in, "I will frail the hell out of you! "While none of us really knew what frail meant, we knew we didn't want it.

"I don't care if it hairlips the devil." I guess it means he really couldn't care less. So the devil, who lives in hell, wakes up one day and says, "I'm not going anywhere today. I have a hairlip! "

"Running true": Dad's way of saying things were level.

"Halmer": Dad's word for hammer.

"Balpine halmer": The best hammer ever made.

"Liloleum": Yes, it's linoleum, but with an *L*. Dad really liked that letter.

"Furlough" Not really a vacation. A word Dad used to say he'd put a stop to something. "I'll put a furlough on that noise!"

"Higher than a Georgia pine": Really drunk, lots and lots of moonshine.

"Fixin' to": About to. "I was fixin' to leave, but I didn't."

"Hellfar": I don't know. I guess how ever far hell is.

"Iota": Not the tiniest, teeniest bit. Not one iota.

"Rolex": What Dad told my husband he bought him for Christmas. "Rolodex": What he really bought him.

"A lick and a promise": Mom's way of saying we hadn't cleaned properly, just swiped at it and promised to come back later and do it right.

"Your lower lip will freeze that way!" and "You'll trip on that lower lip!" Both reserved for Jackie and me only. We were the pouters. It was terribly ineffective. I have no idea why we kept trying it.

"It's easy to be pretty on the outside. It's much harder to be pretty on the inside": Mom's very true words.

"By God, if I have to come up those stairs!" Never good-used by both, always effective.

Dad calls us on the phone very early in the morning: "You up?"
"I am now."

Dad' calls us on our home phones: "Where you at?"
"Umm, at home?"

"Oh my day! "Mom's favorite phrase. Used for everything—shock, surprise, dismay—it covered all areas.

"Every kid needs to eat at least a cup of dirt so they'll be healthy." Mom's words. She believed them wholeheartedly, and now I do too.

"Ducks": What Mom called cigarette butts. We were always disgusted to see Mom's purse filled with "ducks" she'd found on the ground while walking. On the other hand, we spent so much money buying her cigarettes that we were happy if she had some to smoke. She could easily smoke four packs a day, and she'd be even happier with five.

"Until hell won't have it!" Bad! Even hell won't have it, and you don't want it either.

Patty's room has taken on a different, final feeling. Impending death has left a terrible pall. The sobs and Patty's breathing become synonymous. The harder she labors to breathe, the more we sob. Suddenly, we all know why she has waited. Into her room enters Bob, her ex-husband and father to her babies. She has waited for the man who has devastated her financially and emotionally and who ultimately took her children from her. She has waited for him to console her two loves, Buffy and Brad. Even as death waits, she thinks of them first. Now he is here. Now she can go.

# Me

**M**e (Pancake, Waffle). I was the child who worried and fretted over everything. I was terrified of change. I wanted the status quo all the time. For me, it seemed that if things changed, it would only get worse, and I didn't want to take that chance. I was also the one who couldn't tell a lie to Mom when I was young (actually, I got pretty good at it later in life). She'd get the same responses from my siblings; then I'd hear, "Pamela Sue, come here!" Then she'd look at me, and I'd tell her what I'm sure she already knew-the truth. Afterward, I'd have to look at my siblings' faces, and they weren't very happy with me.

Most of my brothers and sisters chewed their fingernails, but JayJay and I probably had the worst-looking nails. Many times we'd chew them so far down they'd bleed. Not only did they look terrible, but they really hurt. Those inner struggles surfaced in so many different ways for all of us kids.

I was happiest when I was playing sports. It didn't really matter which sport; I just loved to play. I will always remember when I turned thirteen. Mom had gone to the little store in town called the D&C (yes, that was really the name), and she bought me a dress. I was grateful because we seldom had money for presents. There were many years when we didn't get anything. It was a pretty dress too, but I had mentioned to my brothers that I really wanted a baseball glove like they had. Somehow Dad managed to take the dress back, and in its place, I got my very own black baseball glove. It was cheap, and when I caught balls, it hurt like hell, but I loved it!

When my sisters and I were old enough, Mom taught us how to sew. Well, actually, she taught my sisters. While they were learning about darts and seams, I was outside with my brothers working on throwing a perfect pass. That worked out just fine too until I had home economics in high school. I had to sew a dress, and I would get my grade for it on the day I wore it to school! Mom was working three jobs at that time, but my neighbor, Alice, helped me. Well, she introduced me to a seam ripper and reminded me that the hem on a dress shouldn't be six or seven inches high. I wore my dress to school, and thankfully, I had that class second period. My instructor told me I'd done a pretty good job, and she gave me a B+. I was thrilled! I still had to make it through the day wearing the dress, however. And, almost immediately, things began to happen. First, the hem fell out. It turns out, I probably should have put those stitches a little closer together; I guess an inch and a half was too much. That darn hem was catching on everything! Then I kept tugging at the underarm of one side because it was too tight. Sure enough, the whole arm fell off! I think I may have used some bad thread on that dress.

Finally, the dismissal bell rang. I started walking as fast as I could to get to the bus, and then I saw her. My teacher was just a step or two behind me, and I was positive she was going to change my grade. I crouched down with my books in hand so she wouldn't notice the hem had fallen out, and I clutched my sleeve and kept it in place with my free hand. I held my breath. The teacher walked right by, and she stopped to talk with another teacher. I jumped on the bus and let out a sigh of relief. The moment I got home, I took that dress off, and then I used my favorite sewing tool—the seam ripper!

I would always ask Mom to let me help her cook or bake. She made me wait for a long time; then one Thanksgiving she said I could make the turkey. That was an honor because our aunts, uncles, and cousins all came that day, and it was a very big deal. First, Mom walked me through the process of cleaning the turkey, taking out the organs packed inside the turkey, and she showed me how to make her stuffing. Mom reminded me of how early I needed to wake up, and I assured her I wouldn't let her down.

I was awake before 5:00 a.m., when Mom always got started, and I went downstairs and started my project. I cleaned the turkey and searched for the organs that should have been inside. There weren't any. I decided they'd forgotten to put them in our turkey, and I continued with making the stuffing. It went into the oven at 6:30, and I was so proud. I just knew it would be the best turkey ever.

When Mom woke up, she started basting the turkey, and she asked where the organs were. I told her there weren't any this time, but she knew better. We took the turkey out, pulled out the stuffing, and there, way in the back, were the organs. Mom started laughing, but I felt bad. She told me no harm had been done, that we didn't need to tell anyone, and that the turkey would be great. I couldn't understand why they'd hidden those organs so far in the back of that turkey and not right up front so you could see them, but Mom was right. No one noticed anything, and the turkey tasted fine.

Connie and I enjoyed working with Dad as he repaired and renovated our house. We learned how to make sure the plywood was "running true" and the proper way to use a "halmer." Dad didn't really know how to remodel or refurbish, but he learned a lot and became quite skilled at reconstructing homes. It was fun carrying around the staple gun and bag of spike nails.

I am the person who always finds the drama in a situation. I happen to believe that life is a continuous drama being played out, not on our televisions but in real time and in real life. This real-life drama cuts me to the core, however, and I am wishing I could stop this somehow—change the channel or turn off the television completely.

# Patty

**P**atty (Pipsqueak, Toothpick) was, what Mom always called, the runt of the litter. She weighed less than eighty-five pounds until she was at least thirty. Patty was the only sibling who wasn't breastfed. Her feisty demeanor more than made up for her lack of poundage, though. She had an inner determination and strength that I admired. From the outside, she looked tiny and frail, but that picture belied her true personality.

Ironically, Patty saved our lives once with her two scrawny little arms. Mom had driven us to our aunt's house, which sat atop a steep and sharp drop of about twenty-five or thirty feet. She left us in the car, and she went in to our aunt's house. Gary leaped from the backseat and grabbed the gearshift, and we began rolling backward, down toward that cliff-like drop. Patty jumped out and held the door open, even as gravity and a whole bunch of kids pulled against her, until Mom ran frantically out and put the car back into gear. She just looked at Gary and shook her head, and then she praised Patty for her quick thinking and strength; it must have been the cod liver oil!

Patty was Mom's ongoing experiment. When Mom wasn't sure what would happen if you left a permanent on your hair too long, Patty showed her, and the rest of us, that it would make your hair ridiculously frizzy. Of course, Mom did it in Patty's teenage years, which made it so much worse for her. That hair could not be tamed even with half a jar of Dippity Do. Speaking of hair and Patty, Mom got very excited when the Batman hairdo became popular, and Patty was there for Mom to give her the cut all the other girls would envy. Patty sat unmoving in the chair until Mom finished the "Batman" bangs. Mom was so proud! She handed Patty a mirror, and we heard her shriek, "Oh no, Mom! The bangs get cut down to a point—not up! "We tried to make her feel better, explaining how quickly bangs grow, but Patty knew we were lying. There was nothing she could do to fix it.

While Patty didn't really enjoy cooking, she loved to iron. And there was always plenty for her to iron. She had a unique way of ironing, though. She always had one foot up and resting on her knee, almost like a flamingo. Patty would stand that way, ironing, for hours on end. Of course, we never said anything because she was ironing all of our clothes.

Patty wasn't into fashion that much, but there was a time when she wore nothing but her white go-go boots. She wore them with everything, and she wore them everywhere. I can't say any more on this subject, however, because I recall begging her to let me borrow them many times.

Patty was a big hit in her freshman year of high school. She made the cheerleading squad, and they just loved throwing her up in the air and catching her because she was so little. She was a Fowlerville Gladiator through and through. She practiced those cheers at home so many times we knew them almost as well as she did. It was Patty, who was so tough and could overcome any obstacle—except for this one.

# Family Life

**B**eing raised poor is pitiful. You find yourself wanting something from almost everyone. I wished I had a new dress. I needed a warm coat; my shoes were falling apart. There wasn't money usually for new shoes; we wore them until they couldn't be worn anymore. Mom always bought only one size of socks: large. When we were little, we had to fold the toes over about halfway down our foot and then put our feet in our shoes. I hated darning socks! We used to put a light bulb down the sock to sew up the holes. Unfortunately, some of us couldn't sew that well (okay, that was me), and the end result was worse than the actual hole.

Since we had so many kids in our family, we were often asked if we were Catholics. It happened so many times I finally started to say, "Yes!" We were, in actuality, Baptists. At least all of us kids were. I think Mom was raised a Baptist, but Dad never really participated in any religion that I'm aware of. He would always take us to church, and then he'd come back and pick us up. He'd be sitting out there, chain-smoking, waiting. Whenever the preacher got longwinded (and it happened often at our church) and kept us later than 12:00, we knew. We would walk out quickly, but he would still scream, "Get your butts in the goddamn car!." Ooh, can I get an *amen*, brother?

Often, we'd see Jehovah's Witnesses come to our door. Dad would always tell us to give them a quarter, take the pamphlet they offered, and then throw it in the trash. One time Patty answered the door. She invited them in, to Dad's chagrin, and told them we were Baptists and how our beliefs differed fundamentally from theirs. She answered each of their arguments with solid Baptist responses. I'm sure they came around occasionally after that, but we were all proud of Patty.

I am grateful to the people in our church back then. They let us know we were loved and appreciated. All that, and they let you sing in the choir too! You didn't even have to audition. However, I came to realize that just because your church lets you sing, it doesn't mean you really can sing. My children remind me of that frequently.

Church carried us through some of the most difficult times in our lives. We went Sunday mornings and evenings, Wednesday evenings, and Mondays for social events when we could. We were Jet Cadets for Jesus/big and strong/living for our Savior/ all day long (we sang that song every Sunday night). We made saltwater taffy, went tobogganing, roller-skating, river rafting, and made trips to the sand dunes. It would be the way we'd be exposed to normal activities. It was our calm in the midst of tumultuous seas.

One year the church paid for Jackie and me to go to summer camp at Camp Cobiac. It was a wonderful, fun-filled week, and we have never forgotten it. Here's the thing about church: you can learn how to live a good, clean life, and you can learn about the importance of giving and sharing, as well as about God, Jesus, and the Bible, and, of course, you can learn how to play strip poker.

Jackie and I were both young, maybe around eleven and twelve, and Connie and Patty were just a few years older when the preacher's son asked us if we wanted to play. We were so naive about stuff like that, but we said yes. We went upstairs to our room, and he taught us how to play. Jackie seemed to be the biggest loser, betting her shirt after losing both her socks and shoes. That is until Mom came upstairs, and then we all became losers. Mom was furious, and she called our preacher. However, when he got there, he placed the blame squarely on our shoulders. He said his son had no idea how to play that game, and we'd obviously encouraged him to participate in our sinful game. Now we did know how to play Setback (Mom and Dad were from West Virginia, and that's a popular game there) and Euchre, but we hadn't known about strip poker. By the way, if you haven't played Euchre, you should try it. It's a very fun and competitive game. Our neighbors, the Tomlins, would take us to Euchre games sometimes at our town hall. They served little sandwiches and fry cakes (plain doughnuts). I don't know if we went for the food or the fun, but we always had plenty of both.

We'd get excited to win anything, even if it was the booby prize.

Many of us were baptized at this church. I was twelve when I decided I wanted to be baptized. I had taken all the required classes; I was ready for my life-altering moment. Ironically, after wading in almost chest-deep water, receiving the official words of the preacher, and having him immerse me backward with a cloth covering my face, I didn't feel much different; I thought I would feel transformed, ethereal. While my fear of choking or coughing hadn't materialized, I believe my epiphany wasn't achieved in part because I had not understood how the same man of God who baptized me could not accept the fact and believe that his son was capable of teaching us strip poker. It didn't make him the worst kid in the world—just human. But it also spoke volumes of our preacher's character too.

After I was baptized, I participated in Communion. I loved it! Not for the unleavened bread or grape juice (at that time Baptists didn't use wine for Communion), but because it made me feel like I had a fresh start, a do-over. Whatever you'd been doing or perhaps hadn't done, you'd give a universal apology and start with a clean slate. What a wonderful gift! I realized in those times that life is a series of learning by mistakes, all the way through it.

We all enjoyed Vacation Bible School too. We memorized Bible verses, learned songs, played games, and essentially discovered ways to grow in our relationships with God. I was terribly frightened of our first pastor. I was very young, perhaps five or six. He would always slam his fist down on the pulpit and yell that we were all sinners and that we were all going to hell. I didn't understand that. Our Dad would yell and scream the same way. He used words like hell and God too, but he usually put "damn it" after or before them. How are you to love a God of whom you are afraid? Can you truly love while you are in fear of someone? I couldn't. I began to imagine God as a huge billowy cloud with a cherubic smile. My sister-in-law Laura, sister to my husband, is a wonderful artist, and she draws those kinds of happy faces with twinkling eyes and bright, engaging smiles. That's what I envisioned.

You can't step back in time, or at least you shouldn't, without acknowledging some humor, laughter, fun—something that helped you survive. The great thing, looking back now, is how very close we all were, except when we weren't. I mean, there were five girls in one bedroom! Linda was the babysitter until the rest of us girls grew up enough to help. Her philosophy at the time was to lock us all upstairs until my parents were due back, and then she'd let us out. It didn't really make any sense to us until we were older and realized there were seven kids to look after, and she never got paid a dime. I'd have locked us up there too!

We froze our butts off all winter long. There was one heater for the whole house, and it was downstairs between the dining room and the living room. It was a coal furnace at first, so we all learned how to shovel coal into a furnace. I hated soot! It was everywhere all the time. After a while, we switched to an oil furnace. That was better. The problem was, however, that at night Dad covered the stairway leading upstairs with a heavy blanket, so none of the heat came upstairs. We could write our names on the inside of our windows. Not to sound gross, but if we fell asleep with a runny nose, we'd have frozen patches on our faces in the morning. It would be those times that we'd pack brothers and sisters in the same bed—and appreciate the body heat!

All of us four girls (Linda was married and living a few minutes away) had chores to do every day. Essentially, there were four jobs: making dinner, washing dishes, drying dishes, and clearing off the table, then sweeping the floor. The easiest job was the last one. Every day, the first person that called their job got to do it. Jackie used to upset all of us because she would wake up, sit up in bed, and yell, "Clear off the table, sweep the floor! "before any of us were even awake.

First of all, just trying to get to sleep proved to be a challenge. We had a little record player upstairs that we played our records on. While we had an assortment that we played during the day, nights were different for us. We always played Floyd Cramer (we all found his music very soothing) or Skeeter Davis (don't really know why, but she helped us fall asleep too). So, on the nights when we weren't huddling in a field or sitting in our neighbors' homes, we were trying to convince our bodies that this night we could and should relax.

Outhouses. Yes, we had one. Dad built our indoor bathroom, but we used that outhouse for a long time before that happened. Of course, there are only two real problems with outhouses: summer and winter. Summer humidity flies—enough said. Now winter wasn't as bad for our neighbors because they had a pot in their bedroom they could use. We didn't have a pot to piss in, literally. Believe me, you had to pee pretty badly to go outside in the middle of the night when it was freezing cold. Our lucky brothers—they could just pee off the front porch!

I wasn't afraid of those holes at our outhouse, but I was terrified of the ones at Parsons School. Most of us went there at least for a few years, but I was there from kindergarten through fourth grade. I walked to school with Ricky, Alice, and Alvin (Alice and Alvin were fraternal twins). Ricky lived on one side of us, and Alice and Alvin lived on the other side. Often, we walked with our other siblings, but the four of us were all in the same grade. Even in those days, it was important to walk carefully in a single-file Indian style. I guess it was about a half mile, but in the winter it seemed much longer. We walked by a haunted house every day. Sometimes Ricky would go up to the door (it was uninhabited—well, except for the ghosts), and he'd swear he heard something walking or moving around, and we would take off running. Mostly we went because rhubarb grew there. It was worth taking a chance on getting spooked for that treat!

Some days we'd all go pick hickory nuts or go look at tadpoles from the twin bridges. We were always confused as to why they called it the twin bridges. First, there was only one, and second, it wasn't really a bridge. Those fall days with the warm sun and leaves changing colors were incredible, and I will always cherish those wonderful memories with my friends. Walking, playing, and being with them every day made life bearable for me.

Mrs. Lepard was our teacher. Alvin, Alice, Ricky, and I were so incredibly fortunate because we had the same teacher from kindergarten through fourth grade. She was, without question, the smartest and most beautiful teacher in the whole world. She taught us Dictionary Detective and Mental Math, but mostly she taught us how to love learning and to value life. She also showed us how to make the greatest cookie in the world: the no-bake cookie.

All eight of us kids were lucky to have aunts, uncles, and cousins that lived fairly close to us. We had Mom's brother, Uncle Junior; his wife, Aunt Lib; Mom's sister, Aunt Jeanette; her husband, Uncle Ang; Mom's sister, Aunt Judy; her husband, Uncle Lemuel; Dad's brother, Uncle Bill; Dad's sister, Aunt Francis, and her husband, Uncle Peck. There was something wonderful about being taken to Flint for a week to be with them. Aunt Lib always played Ray Charles's music, and Aunt Jeanette always let us stay up late to wait with her for Uncle Ang to come home from working the afternoon shift. Uncle Bill was always playing with us, and he made us laugh. Aunt Francis and Uncle Peck were so much fun to be around, and they made us feel very special.

We loved going to their homes. It was there we would learn how families were supposed to be—not perfect, but warm and loving. We'd have huge baseball games where all of our aunts, uncles, and cousins would play at our house. It was always so much fun, and we were able to forget other bad stuff for a while. Our aunts made the best macaroni salad, pies, cakes, and banana pudding in the whole world. But Mom was known for her great cooking also. She always made Thanksgiving dinner, and her stuffing was delicious. Whenever we spent time with our aunts and uncles, we knew we were loved.

As we got older, we all moved to different areas and found work. I'd lived at home for many years, and it was time for me to move. I was almost twenty now, and I needed to experience life on my own. First, I moved to Howell, which was close to my work and not far from our house. I enjoyed having my independence, but I worried about Mom and my brothers. I lived there for several months, and life was somewhat tranquil for a while.

Shortly thereafter, I moved to Brighton, which was closer to my work but quite a distance from the rest of the family. Around this time, Patty and Bob separated, and I was always trying to get Patty to go out partying with me. She really didn't like to drink much then, and she wasn't much at socializing either. I thought my job was to help her with those issues.

I'll never forget one night in March when I picked up Patty in my Camaro. It was about eight at night, and I wanted to go by this guy's apartment that I liked to see if he was home. Well, March in Michigan can be anything from blizzards to floods to sunshine. This particular night, there was a light dusting of snow on the ground; however, we'd had some nice warm weather a few days before. As we pulled into the complex, I saw that his truck was gone. I decided to circle around instead of trying to back out. I drove around what I thought was the parking lot, and suddenly, my car began sinking into the ground! I realized I had driven onto the soggy lawn, and my car was slowly sinking into the mud. True to my character, I quickly became hysterical.

What if he came back and found me here? How was I going to get out? Why did I think this was part of the driveway?

Patty was very upset. "What were you thinking?" she yelled. I told her I was going to push my car out. I found myself wishing I had road service with AAA so I could call and say, "Hello, AAA. Please come and push my car out of the mud before this really cute guy comes back and sees me sitting in the middle of the lawn."

Patty sloshed and squished her way through the mud into the driver's seat, and I got ready to push. I rocked the car, then pushed. Then I rocked it again, more aggressively, then pushed. Again. And again. My car wasn't budging. I was in a full-blown panic, and Patty was getting more and more angry.

"I didn't even want to go out, and you finally convinced me to go, and now I'm stuck! Get in the driver's seat!" she ordered.

I did. Patty rocked the car back and forth, and she pushed it back onto the cement with all eighty-five pounds of her. I was so happy, but I just stammered a "thank you," and off we went. I really wanted to go to the place where I knew the guy would be, but I knew better than to say anything. I let Patty pick the place and kept my mouth shut.

She bailed me out more than once at the bar scene too. I had a nasty habit of flirting with men, then trying to ditch them if they showed interest. One night, on my birthday, we were celebrating at the Holiday Inn with a few friends. I was dancing with this guy who thought I wanted him to rub his genitals up against me repeatedly, and I told Patty that he was a pervert. When the music stopped, the band started calling my name.

"Pam, Pam, we're looking for the birthday girl! "

Everyone pointed at me, standing on the dance floor. The band looked at me and said they were singing the next song for me. I looked around, but my perverted dance partner was gone. I looked at Patty, who was dancing with our neighbor, and I begged her to let me share him with her. She did, but she laughed her butt off the whole time. And, of course, she reminded me once again, in her own very unique and special way, of how I brought these things on myself by flirting and teasing, and I should watch my behavior. I smiled, told her she was right, and I'd try to stop. Of course I didn't.

We had fun in those days, although I knew it was difficult for her. Patty's life had been hard on her. She married Bob at a young age, and she had Buffy shortly thereafter.

Buffy was our own little drama queen, to my delight and Patty's chagrin. It was in stark contrast to Loretta's sedate, calm nature. At first, we weren't sure how to take her. But we fell in love with her stories and songs and her love for life. She was the star of the show, and then Patty got pregnant with Brad. Buffy was four, and she was ready to be a big sister. Bob and Patty were separated during Patty's pregnancy with Brad. She endured a difficult pregnancy, complicated by a cracked rib that brought her unbelievable pain. She'd slipped on a small patch of ice while crossing the street, and the only thing they could do for her was wrap it. I felt so badly for her as I watched her trying to breathe and then getting nauseated and throwing up. She had a cesarean section with Buffy, and another one was planned for Brad. I was going to take Patty on that day and help her through the delivery. Patty, knowing me, continued to ask, "You remember the day, right? Be ready! Are you ready? "

I, exasperated, said, "Yes, Patty, I know the day. I'm not going to mess this up! Stop worrying."

And it was true; I was ready for the date they gave Patty for the cesarean. But I wasn't ready for her to go into labor on April 10, a week before her scheduled date. First, I had a hangover, but I got over that quickly when she called, saying she was contracting a lot and needed to go to the hospital now! I raced the seven miles from the house to Patty's, and I remembered I had no gas in my car. Patty looked like she wanted to strangle me, but she was hurting too much. Bob came and took us to the hospital. It was the fastest ride I've ever taken.

Brad was a tiny little baby, and both Connie and I were thrilled because Mom was in the hospital at the same time with back problems (same hospital too), so we both got to go into the room and see him first. I loved holding him; he just seemed to love being held. I gave him his first bath when Patty brought him home, and he promptly peed all over me. It was worth it, though. He just lay in the water, sleeping. Later, after he'd gone to sleep, I took Buffy shopping. Those were wonderful times, and even though I didn't know it, I was learning how to become a loving, caring mother. I had the best role model possible. Patty's children were her first thought in the morning and the last one at night.

Patty got me through Tom. I had gone through a difficult breakup with my first boyfriend, who had become violent, and I decided I needed a cop to take care of me. I knew he was married and had children, but at the time, I considered that a plus. I knew I didn't want to get married, and I knew he wouldn't ask me, so it seemed right, but of course, it was wrong. I still feel badly about allowing it to go on for so long. I always shared everything about Tom with Patty, and I was grateful because she never judged me on things like that. She just accepted me and loved me anyway.

Some of my favorite times were when I moved to Walled Lake, and Bob and Patty moved across the street not long after. They had reconciled shortly after Brad's birth. Except for the fact I was with a man I didn't love (moved on after the cop), it was a great time. I got to see Brad and Buffy every day, and Patty and I did everything together. We bought roller skates, and we'd skate around the apartment complex together.

I was a bartender and a cocktail waitress at a Holiday Inn, so I worked nights. I was able to spend time doing things with the three of them because Bob left early for work, and he got home pretty late also. They continued to struggle with their marriage, but they were both trying to salvage it.

Patty was actually the person who convinced me to leave Michigan with the professional ballplayer I'd been seeing for a while; I wouldn't have gone. I had a good job, and I was working with a photographer, doing some modeling. Thank goodness I listened. While my relationship didn't work out with the ballplayer, I met my husband here in California. It was difficult living life with a professional sports athlete. We were always traveling. I was never able to work, which is not good for someone like me who'd been used to working since I was seventeen.

I will never forget when I had a huge fight with Sam and I flew home to Michigan. We reconciled almost immediately, so I decided to drive back to California to be with Sam. I had a map that I followed, and I spent the first night in Missouri. I left early the next morning and continued my plan. When I reached New Mexico, I began to panic. There were huge, long expanses of nothingness. Not only were there no cell phones in those days, I couldn't even get any stations on my radio. I started to freak out. Crazy stuff was going through my head. *I'm going the wrong way! I've already passed this town!* Finally, I pulled off and looked for a phone. I was crying hysterically when Patty answered. She talked calmly to me for about an hour, and I was okay by the time we hung up. I drove into beautiful Albuquerque and spent the night there.

The next day, I arrived at Sam's house. Twenty minutes later, we left for LAX, and we flew back to Detroit. When things didn't work out with Sam, I ended up staying out here in California. I stayed with Jackie and Bob, and I got a job at another Holiday Inn, where I met my husband, Mario. Jackie, Mario, and I went to Michigan for Gary and Donna's wedding in 1982. I was apprehensive; I had met Mario's family, and they were normal. Mario's brother, John, was very nice and receptive to me, as was his mother. However, I always say now that it's a good thing I didn't really know Mario's sister, Laura, before I married Mario, because I'd never know for sure if I married him for him or just to be able to call her family. She is such a loving, warm, compassionate, caring person whose spirit manifests itself in everything she does. She is genuine and sensitive, and I'm grateful to know her.

I wondered on that five-hour flight just what Mario would think of my family. I still laugh when I remember how crazy it was. Mario came from a calm, conservative, low-key family. And, uh, we didn't. In retrospect, I guess I should have tried to prepare him, but how? Jackie, Mario, and I stayed at Patty's neighbor's apartment because they were out of town for the weekend. It was perfect because we could spend a lot of time together since we were right next door.

One by one, our siblings flew in. The boys all flew in from Houston, where they were living at the time, and Connie came from Atlanta. Linda lived in Flint, and our parents still lived in Michigan too. And one morning, while Mario and I were lying in bed, the bedroom door opened up, and in walked JayJay! I hadn't seen him in a long time, and I was so happy. First he shook Mario's hand and introduced himself, and then he climbed in bed with us. It seemed pretty natural to me, but Mario just stared at me in disbelief. We just weren't really that modest, I guess.

It was probably Mom's fault, although she couldn't help it. In the summer, spring, and fall, we'd get hosed down outside for our baths, and she'd take us behind the lilac bush to get to the private areas. We actually took our baths in the winter in the kitchen sink, and it was difficult, if not impossible, to show a modicum of modesty. So later, when Mario found his tongue and asked me about it, I explained it the only way I could: "That's how we are."

Gary and Donna had a beautiful wedding, and all of us were there. Mario also couldn't believe that at our weddings, everyone does the hokey pokey. I grabbed him to come up and jump into the circle with me, but he balked, saying, "The hokey pokey—at a wedding?"

"Of course!" I snapped. I don't actually think he did it that night—to my horror. I could just imagine everyone's eyes looking at me, wondering why this stranger refused to do the greatest wedding dance ever created.

When Mario and I decided to get married a year later, I wanted all my family to come. However, we planned it for the following month in Las Vegas, so I knew many of my family and friends wouldn't be able to make it. Gary and Donna flew in from Houston, and Jackie and Bob drove in also. Mario's mom, dad, brother, John, and his wife at the time, Liz, were there, as well as Laura and her husband, Miguel. We were fortunate because Miguel played the guitar and sang in a band, and he serenaded us as we walked through the casino and into the building where our reception would be held. We had many of our close friends there, and it was a great time.

Since Mario owned his own roofing company, we weren't able to go on our honeymoon right away. It worked out well, though, because Gary and Donna stayed with us for a while, and we went many places together and made lots of great memories. We had a wonderful time together, and I'll always be grateful they could spend those days with us.

Almost a month after our October wedding, Mario and I went to Acapulco for our honeymoon, where I got pregnant. By Christmas, I was sick—really sick. Jackie took me to a clinic to make sure I was pregnant, and the test was positive. I called Patty because I was throwing up so violently and so frequently, I was afraid I'd throw the baby up!

"Perfectly normal," she said. "Remember how sick I was?"

"Yes, I do. Okay, okay, I feel better." I knew she would tell me if she thought something else was wrong. The doctor assured me that this was morning sickness.

"Yes, but this is twenty-four hour sickness!" I cried.

"It's fine. It'll stop," the doctor said calmly. And it did. Eventually.

"Hey, Patty, sorry to bother you, but the doctor says the baby is growing on my back. She wants me to do exercises on my hands and knees to make it flip forward. The exercises hurt, and they make me cry. What should I do?"

"Keep doing them, even if they hurt. Remember mine was tipped too, and I had the same problem. It'll be all right."

"Okay, thanks. Sure wish you were here." It seemed just a day or two had passed when I called her again, saying, "Hey, Patty,

I don't want stretch marks. My stomach is getting so big. You know how vain I am!"

"Go buy mineral oil. Put it on every morning and every night on your whole body, not just your stomach. Everything grows. Use old sheets."

"Okay, I will." And I did. And I didn't get any stretch marks with my pregnancies.

When my labor started, I wanted to call everyone because I just knew I was going to have this baby fast and easy. Okay, sure. When it started, it wasn't how the Lamaze instructor said it would be. Instead of every fifteen or twenty minutes, the contractions were every two, three, or four minutes, and they lasted about twenty seconds each time. They started at 10:20 p.m. on a Saturday night, and at midnight I made Mario take me to the hospital. I was certain this baby was about to slide right out of me, and there was no one there to catch it! And, of course, they sent us back home because I was dilated all the way to one.

I spent the next few hours contracting, keeping Mario awake, and wondering how long we should keep doing this before going back to the hospital. I was not about to name my firstborn child after a taxi or ambulance driver, so at 4:00 a.m., we went back to the hospital. The nurses kept telling me to sleep between contractions. That was impossible because sometimes not even a minute passed between the contractions. I knew I was in unfamiliar territory because I wanted my mom desperately. For so long, all of us had become like mothers to her, and I found this turn of events frightening.

Jackie stayed there the whole time, though, and I was extremely grateful. Never having had a child, Jackie was pretty much like me scared to death. I know they could hear me screaming all the way down the hall, but she still stayed and waited. At 8:30 p.m., we had Malina. One look at her, and I knew everything I'd gone through had been well worth it. She was this amazingly beautiful little doll. We left the hospital a day and a half later. I called Patty the moment I walked into the house.

"She sounds so cute!" she said when she heard her cry. I thought so too—at first!

"Malina's crying so hard, and she's not wet or hungry."

"Turn her over your knee and rub her back. She probably has gas.

"Okay, I'll try." Before long, I needed to call her again, saying, "Patty, Malina's almost five months old. She almost rolled over today. Is that fast, slow, or just right?"

"Malina's going to do things in her own time. Don't worry about when everyone else's kid did it. Just enjoy her—it goes very fast."

In the meantime, Patty was facing terrible struggles. No money. Evictions. She really had it rough. We all tried to help her financially, but every time she'd get a little break, someone or something would trip her up again. When I became pregnant with Angela, things really began to spiral downward for Patty. We talked all the time because I had many problems with Angela, including several times when the doctor said I was going to miscarry. Even though Patty had so much on her plate, she always found time to console or listen to me. Mario and I were so afraid we were going to lose Angela, and just talking with Patty relaxed me and helped me cope. When she was born, it was like a tiny miracle to us. She was a quiet, cuddly little darling that developed and blossomed just perfectly. We knew we'd been blessed twice.

Shortly thereafter, we knew things had taken a turn for the worse for Patty, She, Buffy, and Brad were living in one room, and oftentimes they only had popcorn to eat for dinner. Patty desperately tried to keep them together. She worked as much as she could, doing anything she possibly could. Toward the end, they were living out of Patty's car. Unfortunately, the apartment managers would always base Patty's rent on what she made and what Bob was supposed to pay for child support. Since that money wasn't forthcoming, she continued to be evicted from place after place. Still, she persevered; she had the two loves of her life, and she was all right. Eventually, Bob, who had remarried, took Buffy and Brad from Patty. He told them in court he couldn't pay the back child support he owed, but he offered to have them live with him. He offered stability, which Patty was unable to provide, through no fault of her own. That move took the life out of Patty. It crushed her heart and her soul. Her reason for living had been yanked from her. It was devastating.

I brought Patty out to California because I believed she'd suffered a breakdown. I was frightened that she would do something to herself. Patty was a complete mess, inconsolable. I didn't push her to do anything because I had no clue what she was going through. I did take her to Newport Beach. I don't know if she remembered it at the time, but if there was something to help her find a way to want to keep living, it would be there. She stayed with us for a while, and eventually she found some peace and resolved to keep going. We were satisfied with that, all things considered. It was enough, for now.

I tried to convince her to stay here in California, get a job, and go to school, but I already knew she wouldn't. She had to go back to Michigan; her two children were there. I would have gone too. It was very emotional when she left, and we were worried for her. Bob lived in Fowlerville, which was fortunate, as Patty found a job and a place to stay there as well. Both Brad and Buffy experienced so much difficulty not having their mom with them every day. They hadn't lived with their dad for a long time either, so this transition was tough.

Buffy, perhaps because she was older, took it much harder. Just a few months after moving in with Bob, she became pregnant. I remember getting the call from Patty and feeling so sad for them both. Buffy didn't want to tell Bob, and Patty didn't force her. So we arranged for Buffy to leave her home as if going to school, and Patty would put her on an Amtrak for California.

It was March, and Buffy was halfway through the pregnancy. When Buffy got off the train, I tried to prepare her for absolute, utter chaos. She knew Mario from Gary and Donna's wedding, so she met Malina and Angela. Malina was five and in kindergarten, and Angela was two. Our parents had come out for a visit two years earlier, and they never left. In fact, they moved into our rental home right next door to us. It was a duplex, and they lived on one side. JayJay had come to California in January, and he was living in the other apartment of the duplex.

We also had our roofing company at our home, so every morning we'd hear the employees and smell the trucks and tar pots. Since I did the office work, there was an office inside our home as well. The phones started ringing early in the morning and continued until late in the evening.

Malina struggled terribly with asthma also, and many nights I sat up with her, holding the nebulizer to her mouth and nose so she could breathe. Mario and I were lucky to have a wonderful pediatrician, though, who was also our good friend. He was always available to help us get through those unbelievably frightening times, and we will forever be grateful.

Thankfully, Buffy was accustomed to change, and she adapted well. While I would have never wished this pregnancy on her, having her out here was so special. I could talk to her about how Mom and Dad were driving me crazy, and she would totally understand. JayJay, Buffy, and I would sit together and just laugh our butts off a lot. Nobody can imitate our mom like Buffy. She would pretend to smoke a cigarette just as Mom did, and her southern drawl was perfect. Buffy actually did Mom for Mom once, and Mom cracked up laughing. Mom did not know that Buffy was pregnant, however. We just weren't sure how she'd react if she knew that Buffy was going to give the baby up for adoption. Fortunately, Mom didn't notice a lot of things, and Buffy wasn't a tiny thing to begin with, so it worked out.

Once we were sure Buffy was serious about her intent to give up the baby, we set out trying to get things in order for that to happen. Buffy turned eighteen while she was here, but she was still so young. It was a scary time for Buffy, and she called Patty often. It got closer to her due date, and Mom and Dad drove back to Michigan. Dad knew all about it, and our plan was for them to go to Michigan and bring Patty back with them after the baby was born and with its new family. Then Patty and Buffy would fly back to Michigan together.

What we hadn't prepared for, as we should have, was that this little guy was not going to be rushed! Jayjay drove Buffy around in our big work truck over bumpy roads for a while—nothing. She took something that was supposed to get the contractions started—nothing. By then, Dad couldn't stall anymore, and he, Mom, and Patty left for California. Buffy's obstetrician induced her the next day. She labored for a long time, with no results. Buffy ended up needing a caesarian, and the new parents whisked the little guy off almost immediately. Patty arrived at the hospital later that evening, and Buffy was happy that her mom was here with her now.

While I may be writing this in a matter-of-fact way, the reality and magnitude of this were anything but. Buffy did the right thing for the baby, but it was absolutely the hardest thing in the world for her. A piece of her was gone and would become a part of a different family. We were immensely grateful that he began his life in a loving home, but our hearts hurt. Patty felt guilty, and she wished she could have done more. She wished she had a good job, a decent home, and a future. Mom was told that Buffy had an emergency appendectomy, and she was in the hospital.

"What good timing," Mom said, "that Patty just happened to come back with us!"

When Buffy was released from the hospital, she and Patty spent a few more days with us. We went to the Queen Mary, the movies, and then we had a farewell party. It was so hard to have them leave, although we all knew they couldn't stay. I was very proud and happy for Buffy, though. First, she completed her GED out here in California during her pregnancy, and that was difficult. And when she and Patty flew back home, she moved in with Patty. It was quite a way for Patty to get her child back, but at least she was back with her, where she belonged.

Bob learned about the pregnancy, and eventually everyone was back on speaking terms. We were all glad for that. There simply wasn't time or energy for any more bad feelings.

Brad continued to stay with Bob. But life for Patty had become a little more normal, however short-lived. Patty's boyfriend, Mike, brought her many problems. I don't think she ever knew for sure if he was married or not. He was a drunk, but he was also a man who took Patty on trips, as well as Buffy and Brad, and, in those lean years, he sometimes provided food for them. Perhaps that's why it took her so long to sever those ties with him. We are appreciative of him, however, for all the pictures he took of Patty. Many of them were incredibly beautiful.

I think several of us kids struggled to end relationships, perhaps due to our own insecurities. I didn't like to talk to him, ever. My gut told me more about him than Patty did, and she had shared quite a bit. I was so happy and proud of Patty when she cut that loser out of her life for good. I took some perverse pleasure in knowing that he had begged and pleaded with Patty to take him back. What goes around, I believe, will come back around.

I called Patty often on Sundays. I would be ironing, and we would catch up. I'd complain about how hard it was having Mom and Dad next door, and then I'd regale her with stories about the many wonderful and exciting things my girls were doing. I would take Mom to her regular physician several times a month and to her psychiatrist much more frequently. It was unbelievably hectic, and I often felt overwhelmed.

My girls loved going over to Grandma and Papo's house, though. Malina had called Dad "Papo" since she was one, and it stuck. One year, Mom made Angela an Ariel costume from The Little Mermaid. She did a great job, and Angela was thrilled. When Mom was good, she was really good, but when she wasn't, Patty just listened and empathized.

Before they moved out to California, they had moved in with her. She totally understood. Mario and I bought a new home a few miles from where we were, and we were elated. Mom and Dad still lived in the duplex, but we had some privacy at last. We had terrific neighbors, a great school with a wonderful teacher for Malina, and life was good.

Patty worked and worked. She'd tried to work at Walmart and other places too, but they used her, then dumped her. For some time, Patty had been having problems with her arm. She often had trouble lifting or even moving it, but still, she worked. She'd get her shot of cortisone, and back to work she'd go.

Buffy had settled in and was working too, but she endured yet another tragic event in her life. She had become pregnant again, but this time, the child died inside her during her ninth month. It was unbelievable. How could God be so cruel to do this? There was no way to understand. Buffy was forced to labor, giving birth to her dead son. She named him Jared. It was sad beyond words.

Patty was a rock throughout the ordeal. She convinced Buffy to hold him and say good-bye. I don't know how she stayed so strong. It is a testament to many things, probably the biggest being her love for her children. They buried the little angel, and Buffy tried once again to pick up the pieces of her life.

Patty worked at the Bloated Goat Tavern in Fowlerville. She struggled so much because she would cook the food as well as serve it, and she would make and serve drinks also. She hurt all the time now, and not just in her arms. The doctor gave her some medicine to go along with the cortisone shots for the pain.

We had added a little something to our family about this time. We were blessed with a son, Aaron. He was the part of our family we'd been missing. When I held him for the first time, he opened one eye and winked at me as he wrapped his tiny hand around my finger. Angela turned nine a week after he was born, and Malina was eleven. They were wonderful with him, and they still are. This little darling has had not one but three little mothers to care for him. They helped feed and change him, and all of us marveled at his accomplishments. He was precious and precocious, adventurous, busy, and very loving.

When Buffy fell in love with Roger, we met them in Las Vegas. Loretta, Patty, Brad, Buffy, Roger, Jackie, Bob, Mario, Malina, Angela, Aaron, and I made the trip. I knew Buffy truly cared for him, and it was clear he loved her too. The two of them talked about marriage, but Patty had some doubts. I totally understood. She'd watched Buffy go through so much, and marriage was a risky venture. I think we all knew, though, when we parted that day that a wedding was forthcoming. And it was.

We knew months in advance, and we began preparing. Mom and Dad were going, and Jackie and I were taking my three children. All the brothers and sisters were trying to make it in for the wedding. We put Mom and Dad on a train a few nights before we were scheduled to leave. The train was great, though. The girls enjoyed the scenery, and Aaron ran everywhere, all the time. We had done the unthinkable—we took a two-year-old on a two and a half-day trip across the United States!

Michigan was wonderful. It was great to be home. We met Trevor (Loretta's son), who was about four, and Branden (Roger's son from a previous marriage), who was about three, and all of us were able to reconnect.

Buffy's wedding was perfect. She isn't the formal type, thank goodness, but it was heartfelt, sincere, and lovely. Buffy had asked Malina and Angela to walk in her wedding, and that made the evening even more special.

*Buffy and Roger's wedding,*
*From Left: Brad, Roger, Buffy and*
*Patty, Branden stands proudly in front of his dad.*

Even though I know technically the gathering after the wedding is called a reception, we had a party. There was dancing, drinking, drinking, dancing, and we made lots of memories.

*This is the last picture of all of us together.*
*Taken at Buffy's wedding.*
*From left: Darryl, Me, Jackie, Gary, Dad,*
*Mom, Linda, Connie, Patty and Jayjay*

After the reception, several of us went to The Bloated Goat. All of the brothers and sisters—except for Linda, who had a long distance to drive home—and Loretta went into one of the hotel rooms where many of us were staying. My girls, Stephanie (Gary and Donna's daughter), and Aaron stayed in our room. We had the time of our lives in that room. We did angel balances and butt balances, talked, laughed, and just enjoyed each other. I think, for Patty, she could finally relax after months of preparing for the wedding and reception. Thank God we had those moments together. I don't think any of us will ever forget that night.

The next morning, we all had breakfast together. Linda and Rich drove down, and Uncle Ang came too. He came to say goodbye to Connie, Darryl, Jayjay, Gary, Donna, and Stephanie because they all had to leave. We loved being around Uncle Ang anytime, all the time. They left, and we were sad but extremely grateful we'd been able to spend time and make memories together. Mom, Dad, my kids, Jackie, and I stayed in Michigan a few more days, and Patty, our tour guide, took us to the Fowlerville Fair, Greenfield Village, and Canada. But the best thing we did, by far, was eat at Aunt Jeanette and Uncle Ang's house. My girls told me later they really hadn't believed me when I told them about the best banana pudding in the world and potato salad too! To this day, Malina and Angela remember that meal: burgers, potato salad, and banana pudding. We sat outside in their backyard and just relaxed.

I loved being there. It always made me feel peaceful and content, and this time was no exception. Uncle Ang brought out the Slip 'n Slide, and Aaron—was ready to go! Of course, we hadn't brought him any trunks, so with Uncle Ang's sly grin and a nod of his head—Aaron dropped his shorts and underwear, and he took off! We had a good laugh and some compromising pictures of my darling son. It was hard to leave Michigan. I remember Brad sitting with Aaron on the bench as we waited, and I thought about how much I wanted them to always know each other and be close. Brad was so helpful and sweet, and I knew he would be a great role model for my children. I just wanted to grab him and take him with us. In spite of all the obstacles Patty faced, she had raised two beautiful, caring, hardworking, loving kids. She should be, and was, so very proud.

After Buffy's wedding, Patty's health really began to deteriorate. Her muscles hurt constantly, and we began to hear the word fibromyalgia. She still worked at The Bloated Goat, but I knew she was suffering. To add to her problems, she didn't have any health insurance, and everything cost so much money. That's the catch-22 that so many people are caught in where no one would take her because of her preexisting condition, but she couldn't heal that preexisting condition because she couldn't afford it.

We managed to have some fun with Patty through those times, however. Shortly after Buffy's wedding, Buffy, Roger, Branden, and Patty came to California for a visit. We had a blast! Roger rented a car, and we went to Mexico. It was beautiful. We shopped, ate, and went to a lovely beach. Clean, beautiful sand, the ocean in front of us, and an incredibly blue sky created an amazing memory for us there. I remember walking with Patty on the beach and thinking again how I wished she would move here and be close to the beach and the ocean. It seemed to be cathartic. It possessed some healing properties for her.

On the way back across the border, my children got to see how much fun their Aunt Patty could be. As we waited in line to cross, with Roger, Buffy, Patty, and Branden in the car behind us, we saw many young children singing, selling gum, and doing anything they could to make a little money. We bought gum and lots of other stuff we clearly didn't need. To our surprise, Patty was cleaning our windshield and singing at the same time. We just cracked up; she totally caught us off guard!

Later, I brought up her desire to be a teacher's aide to work with handicapped children. "They're hiring out here! "I said, even though I didn't know if they were.

"I would, but I don't want to leave my kids and my grandkids," she answered.

And I understood. While she didn't live vicariously through her children, her role in their lives was clear, unmistakable, and permanent. "We're going about this the wrong way," I added. "Let's talk them into moving out here."

She responded, "Buffy might, but I don't know about Brad. He loves his hunting. He already got one deer with his gun, and now he's going to try for one with the bow and arrow." There was no mistaking the pride in her voice. She was proud, not just of their accomplishments, but of their attempts to try new things, to add different dimensions to them. And I was proud too—proud to be connected to them and to Patty. I truly believe the sun, the ocean, and no humidity all helped Patty feel better. Although I never doubted for a moment she was genuinely ill, she seemed so much healthier out here.

Right around this time, Brad and Nikki decided to marry. They had a small ceremony, but it was beautiful and heartfelt. Patty loved Nikki, and she was happy for both of them.

Patty has a great love for animals. Her dog, Dakota, was her baby. Whenever Patty was out here visiting, our dogs would always try to get close to her. She let them climb in her lap, and Brandy, our poodle, would always have to sleep with her. She didn't mind. She would call after she left many times and ask, "Have you guys been lovin' on Brandy? She needs a lot of attention."

Patty is a wonderful grandmother. She and Branden are very close. When they came here on that trip to California and Mexico, Branden looked for Patty every minute. If she was in another room, he had to go find her. It was special and sweet. Patty always told me how much she loved watching Tyler and Jorden. She raved about what good little guys they are, and after meeting them, I knew she wasn't just grandma-talking. They really are great little guys. It's no wonder all of us fell in love with them.

One year, Patty, Connie; Darryl; his wife at the time, Joy;

Seara, Darryl's daughter; Loretta; and her son, Trevor, came out for a visit. We had a great time with everyone. We went to Patty's favorite, Newport Beach, for the day and Chuck E. Cheese. Everyone spent time with Mom and Dad, and we all made some great memories.

Malina graduated from high school in 2002, and Patty and Connie came out for her party. It went perfectly. Patty made chocolate-covered strawberries, and Connie made margaritas. Both were big hits, and the few days they were here flew by.

**B**uffy and Roger decided they were going to try to add to their family. It took some time, but one day Patty called and said they were finally pregnant. Patty was thrilled, and I was too. Branden was about to become a big brother. We all knew he was going to be a good one. Patty kept me abreast of the pregnancy, and we celebrated each milestone. Unfortunately, Buffy had suffered a miscarriage earlier in their marriage. This was compounded by the fact it happened on the same day she'd given her son up for adoption years before here in California. It was a shock, and Patty wondered how much her daughter was supposed to handle. We all prayed this pregnancy would go well, and we were glad as we came closer to Buffy's due date.

When Jacob was born early, he had some problems, and he stayed in the hospital. Patty was worried, but she only shared it with me. She kept reassuring Buffy that everything would be fine. And it was. He is just the cutest little fellow. We watched him learn something new every day. He is bright, precious. Meanwhile, Patty had begun working at Wranglers, a bar and grill just a few miles from her home. She has a terrific boss, Angela, who has helped Patty in every possible way from day one. Patty and Angela are very close. Buffy works there also, so Angela knows the family well.

Wranglers was closed between Christmas and New Year's, which was great because Patty could come visit us. She never had the money to fly, but Connie would use her frequent flier miles so she could come. Having Patty during that time was the greatest. Aaron's birthday is the day after Christmas, so the first year she was able to come to his party. Unfortunately, on top of the fibromyalgia, she'd been experiencing vertigo. That first year, it was just a small problem. The doctors had been running tests, and they were inconclusive as to it being perhaps vertigo, maybe Meniere's disease.

From that year to the next was unbelievable in terms of how her health deteriorated. She missed a lot of work. She couldn't even stand up some days. It seemed to affect her every other day for some reason. She went back to the doctor. More tests. Patty was given steroids for her ears. She was being treated for Meniere's disease, but there had been no change in her symptoms. At some point, she had a brain scan. The neurologist said she had some white spots on her brain, but he was not concerned about them. We all freaked out when she told us.

"What do you mean he's not concerned about them?" I asked her. "They clearly don't belong there, and with all the other problems you're having..." I shouldn't have said that because I knew it was so much scarier for her.

"I know. It really bothers me. I don't know what to do. I have to save my money for more tests. I'm filling out paperwork to get assistance from the state, but it takes time."

Patty's symptoms became much worse. She deliberated about coming to California the following Christmas because she was so dizzy. I was torn because I wanted her to come so badly, but I know planes and ears and dizziness do not mix. She decided to come. Patty was awfully sick when she got off the plane. She was very sick and very dizzy. We felt so badly for her. She just cried and cried; so did we. She stayed with us for eight days, most of which were spent in bed. She barely ate, and the worst possible thing happened to Patty: she could not read anymore because of the dizziness. She had always been a voracious reader. She'd read anything, everything. Every night she read to help herself fall asleep, and now she couldn't. This was horrible. The one small thing to give her some quality of life was taken from her too.

She had a return ticket on the twenty-ninth of December, and she and I left for the Ontario airport. Patty didn't feel well at all. By the time we made that twenty-five minute drive, she was sick and dizzy. We got out, and she crumbled by the car. She sobbed and sobbed, and I joined her. "I can't take this! I can't live this way! Why won't it stop? God, please make it stop!" Then she got sick.

I almost called 911. I didn't know how to help her. In retrospect, I wish I would have. Maybe they would have given her another brain scan, and this time maybe they wouldn't dismiss it as "nothing to worry about." I called a doctor friend of mine, and he suggested we call her doctor in Michigan. We did, and he prescribed some medication for her. She took it for a few days, and then she went back to Michigan. She made it back all right, but to this day I wish I had done something different—anything. That ended up being the last time I would see her when she was walking and talking.

Life continued to get harder and harder for her to live. At one point, she told me her grandchildren were giving her a reason to live. Patty had met her match; she was up against something beyond terrible. She repeated these statements to us: "I saw the same doctors; they gave me the same tests and the same medications, and I got the same results." Patty got worse. Now it wasn't every other day. Now it was most days. Sometimes she'd collapse because they gave her diuretics to try to keep fluid from pooling in her ears, and it dehydrated her. They would hydrate her and then release her. I urged her to drive to Ann Arbor and have Buffy or Brad run in, asking for a wheelchair, and saying Patty had collapsed. I hoped that by doing that they'd run more sensitive, comprehensive tests and properly diagnose her.

Turns out, they didn't need to fake it; she collapsed and was taken to Ann Arbor. Unfortunately, all they did was hydrate her and release her again. So the looming, white, "they're-no-problem" spots on her brain continued to make Patty's life a living hell. She went through so much paperwork to get financial help from the state. It is infuriating when you think of the millions of people who work their butts off with low-paying jobs who simply cannot afford health insurance. And while all of her siblings could help a little, no one could absorb that type of cost. Patty's life consisted of trying to work, going to the doctor, trying new medications, and crying.

For about the past year, when I called Patty, I left messages. She was simply too overwhelmed to talk, and oftentimes she was unable to even call me back. I understood, and I began to call less and less. She knew I loved her, and I knew she was just too sick to do almost anything. She needed to save her energy to try to work and live. Patty also knew I would be at the airport in a heartbeat to pick her up if she wanted to come out to California. Most of the time, I spoke with Buffy.

"Mom's back in the hospital. She collapsed. They're giving her fluids, and then they're going to release her. Brad and I keep telling them they need to do more tests, but they are letting her go."

I said, "Oh my God, what are they trying to do—kill her?"

I felt so sorry for Brad, Nikki, Buffy, and Roger. They were going through hell. We all vented our frustration at a poorly run health organization and at our inability to help, being so far away. When I got the call about Patty collapsing again and them taking her back to Ann Arbor, I was relieved. This time, probably because she had deteriorated so much since the last time they had released her, several tests were run. As I play it back in my mind, it's all a blur. The diagnosis was brain cancer. They would begin radiation and chemotherapy immediately. First, they measured her head to fit her for some type of protective mask. The plan was for her to go home and travel back and forth to Ann Arbor for the radiation and chemotherapy. That was the plan. She would stay at Buffy's home.

She spent her last Thanksgiving in Ann Arbor. Buffy said she had eaten, and family and friends had visited. I called, and Patty was resting. Buffy asked if I wanted to talk to her anyway, but I said no and that I would talk to her later when she was at Buffy's. I could kick myself now because I never had another conversation with my sister where she was able to speak directly to me. I'd give anything to go back and tell Buffy that I wouldn't bother her for long, but I just wanted to hear her voice.

Patty was discharged, and we began to plan our trip home to Michigan. The doctors had given her a year to live with the radiation, and it had shocked and devastated all of us. Only a year, oh my God, only a year to live! We knew if they said a year, we might only have about six months or so with our sister.

Patty didn't do well at Buffy's. She was extremely disoriented, and they took her back to Ann Arbor. The day she was to begin radiation, she lapsed into a coma. While they were admitting Patty back into the hospital, she asked. Buffy if I had gotten the flowers she'd had Buffy send me for my birthday. When Buffy told me, I completely fell apart. I could not believe with her whole life literally crumbling around her, she had remembered me. It was a moment that I will cherish forever.

Almost immediately, Connie called me at work to say there would be no radiation, no chemotherapy. They'd found another tumor in her esophagus; she had a week to live. Unable to take Mom now, Mario took Jackie and me to the airport. I left my three children huddled in a bed together, crying. I tried to be strong, at least for now. I didn't know how to deal with life without Patty. Malina was halfway through her pregnancy. Who could I talk to now about being a grandma? I had so many things to ask her about. She was such an amazing grandma. As Jackie and I went through security at the airport, a bird flew down the long hallway. We both looked at each other and gasped. Whenever a bird flew inside a home or building, Mom used to say someone was going to die.

Patty's breathing is rattled and labored. The room is filled with people, yet that is the only sound. We are all waiting. I still believe that God can undo this; I believe in His power. He could heal Patty just like he did with Lazarus. The hospice nurses come in and tell us that Patty could stop breathing briefly and resume breathing again. This could be a process, but maybe not. Connie is on one side of Patty's bed. I am on the other. Roger is holding Buffy, and Bob stands with Brad. Everywhere there is sobbing. No, no, no, this cannot be happening. Don't let her go, please, God. We need her. It seems surreal, as though we are not really there, but we are. We know we are experiencing death together.

Patty appears to be choking; the nurses offer suction. We decide against it. The few moments Patty struggles to breathe are horribly, interminably long. Okay, okay, God, just take her. Let her go. Please, dear God, let her go. Patty stops breathing. We are crying hysterically. Nurse enters. No. Patty still has a pulse. She needs to stop breathing for a full minute. We wait. This time her breathing is shallow, almost quiet. She stops breathing again. We wait. We wait and wait; she does not start breathing again. Our beloved sister, mother, aunt, daughter, grandma, and friend are gone. Now we can let it all out; we can cry.

We all leave the room and allow the nurses time to prepare her. Some of us go out one door, while others go to the side of the hospital. I walk outside. Buffy is crying hysterically in the arms of the hospice nurse. She needs to do this; she has been strong for a very long time. Some of us are sitting. I am standing with JayJay. We walk a few steps into the cold Michigan air. It is late in the evening, and JayJay and I look up into the dark sky for an answer, an explanation, some kind of reason. Help us understand why someone who's been through so much in her lifetime had to go through that too. As if on cue, we look toward the heavens, and suddenly, these huge, beautiful, sparkly white snowflakes fall on us. They were enormous, magical. Through our tears, JayJay and I look at each other and smile. She was alright; she was in God's hands now.

We said our final good-byes, and Patty was taken away. She had said she wanted to be cremated. All of us went to Buffy's that night, and we drank. I do not know how many beers I drank, but it was a lot. There was such a need in us to release everything we'd been bottling up, and we did. Nine days had passed from the day Jackie and I flew in, but it seemed like one very long day and night.

We began early the next morning preparing for Patty's funeral. It would be on Saturday, December 9, and we'd have a visitation on Friday, the 8th. Jayjay and I took some pictures to a video guy who said he could have it ready by the next day. The service for Patty would be in Fowlerville, and there would be food after at Wranglers. JayJay and I went by The Bloated Goat and let them know of Patty's passing. Buffy and our friend, Tina, made food for all of us too. We love her so much. We all are grateful to know she'll be there for Buffy. Her heart will suffer without Patty also.

We are deciding on music. Patty's friend, John, will sing "In the Garden," and Darryl will recite a poem. Roger had gone to Walmart for picture frames to have at the visitation. When he returned, he told us how a Salvation Army person had their bucket in front of the store. Roger dug into his pocket and pulled out his loose change. He said he tossed it all in, but one coin didn't go in. When he picked it up, he discovered it was a coin that Patty had given him some time earlier. We all believe that was Patty's way of telling him she'll be watching out for them. Jayjay shared how oftentimes people who have passed will leave coins out in the open for us to find. It was nice to hear that; we hoped it would happen to us too.

Thursday evening, after dinner, some of us went to Wranglers. We were surprised to see all the Christmas decorations, especially when we saw Patty's name, along with the other employees, written in sprayed snow on the refrigerator. We could feel her in there with us. Angela brought over a round of shots of Tequila Rose. We stayed there much later than we meant to, and we all got a little closer to Angela too.

The day of the visitation, we were all dressing at Buffy's when my cell phone rang. It was Malina.

"Mom," she said excitedly, "I'm having a girl!" Life was continuing after death. Amazing.

We had two visitations on Friday, with a two-hour break between them. Most of us had never met Kaylee, Ronnie's daughter. She is fourteen and just the sweetest little thing. She spent a lot of time with Patty, and she and her mom cried with us at their loss as well. She looked so scared and sad; we all just wanted to hug her. We cried with friends and family and people we didn't know, and we left, drained.

The next day would be even harder, we knew. Our brothers, Connie, and I had gone to Patty's trailer to pack up her things. We knew it would be too difficult for Brad and Buffy. JayJay was a mover for a living, so he showed us the best and fastest way to wrap her things.

As we boxed up Patty's entire life, we tried to take a few special things as a remembrance for the family. Patty loved Indian things; they were everywhere. I decided to keep several hematite stones, one for everyone in my family and my granddaughter. I also kept a small Indian headdress. One of the parts was broken, and it was being held together with a large safety pin. Jayjay offered to fix it, but I wanted it just the way it was.

We brought several things for Brad and Buffy, and then we left. Dakota (Patty's dog) was staying with Brad now, but the son of one of Patty's dearest friends who'd passed away some time earlier decided he would stay at Patty's trailer. He loved Patty dearly; this would be a hard thing for him to do.

Saturday morning was a beautiful, crisp, big, billowy- cloud day. It was December, but it seemed more like spring on this day. Just a few days ago, there had been lots of snow and ice too. We gathered at the funeral home, and we prepared ourselves to say a final good- bye. The preacher was the same man who'd spent time with us at Medilodge, and he had stayed with us until almost the very moment she passed. He recounted some of the stories we had shared with him in those earlier days.

When he asked if anyone wanted to speak, I stood up. I shared Patty's love for her children and grandchildren, Newport Beach, and how difficult it would be for us to leave Brad and Buffy. I clutched Patty's Indian headdress as I spoke, and I felt her spirit with me. There were many people there, some from Wranglers and The Bloated Goat. I told everyone I felt like she was walking in the sand at the beach, unbelievably healthy, moving slowly away from all of us, smiling and waving, ethereal-like. The front of this book's picture is what I kind of imagine with Patty, although it was actually a double exposure from a picture taken of her some time ago.

Darryl made it through the poem, but it was tough for him. John, who sang for us, was also one of the kindest people we'd met. He and his wife, Barb, were so considerate and helpful to us during our time at Medilodge. We will never forget them; we will forever be grateful. John struggled a bit at the end of the song, and our hearts ached with his. We couldn't believe this was the end—her end. We'd been doing so many things so fast since we'd gotten here; we hadn't really accepted the finality of it all. Reality smacked us all in the face, hard.

Patty's ashes were not there for the funeral. We had rushed to have the service before we all had to leave, so those would be given to Buffy and Brad later. After the service, as we embraced each other, I looked at the crowd. I saw my dear friend, Alice, and I couldn't believe it. None of us thought many of our friends would make it since it had all happened so quickly. We hadn't been able to notify very many people. I hugged her and told her how surprised and happy I was to see her. Lorene (her sister) and their mom came also. It was nice to have them with us. All of us talked to everyone there, but I kept gravitating back to my childhood friends. I'd always been able to talk to Alice, and I took comfort in having her there.

We all left the funeral home and drove to Wranglers. Many people joined us there, including Uncle Jimmy and his wife, Uncle Bill (Dad's brother), and many of Bob's brothers and their families, and we had lots of drinks too. We began saying good-bye and making our way out of Wranglers. We were going to Brad and Nikki's home. They lived just a few minutes from there. They have a beautiful home, and we felt Patry's spirit everywhere. Brad, the hunter, had a few deer heads mounted and displayed. All of his aunts and uncles were proud as we looked at his conquests. We took many pictures, and then we said good-bye to Connie, her friend, Jay, Darryl, Gary, Donna, and Stephanie. That proved to be a difficult task. Suddenly, we were all going our separate ways. We'd been together for a while now, every minute of every day, and it was hard imagining not seeing them every day.

Jayjay would ride to the airport with Jackie and me and then head back to Idaho. His flight to Boise left about the same time ours did, at 6:00 am. We went back to Buffy's, and Brad said they'd be over later. I started mentally preparing myself to go home to California. My heart was in California, but it was here in Michigan too. I knew Roger would take care of Buffy and Brad and Nikki would get through too, but still...

When Brad left Buffy's that night, we were all crying. All of a sudden, he was a little boy to me again, and I needed to take care of him. I desperately wished at that moment that we all lived in California, so I could see them all the time. We probably did the smartest thing for Buffy and us; we got up at 3:00 am., wrote notes, and left without waking them. It was devastatingly sad. I had to keep concentrating on the drive and getting to Metro Airport. We made it there, and JayJay left to catch his plane. Then it was Jackie and me, as it had been from the start.

"It feels so weird," I told Jackie. "How can we leave them all here, but how can we not leave?"

She responded, "I know what you mean. I feel the same way."

It was pitch-black when our plane took off. We tried to rest, but we really couldn't. We talked on the way, and the plane made a stop in Arizona. We had about an hour left on our flight to California. I felt better when we took off from there. Even though I'd been in constant communication with my family, I'd missed them terribly, and I was so anxious to see them. The sky was beautiful and blue all the way, and Jackie and I were counting the minutes. Then Jackie saw it. She kept trying to show me something outside of the window, but I couldn't see it.

"Where? Where? I don't see anything!" I kept repeating.

The man behind me yelled, "I see it! Wow! I fly all the time, and I have never seen anything like this!"

We were beginning our descent, and I still couldn't see it. Jackie kept trying to show me where to look so I could see it. And finally, I saw it. To this day, I want to cry when I remember it. It was a tiny version of our plane, enclosed in a circle of rainbow colors. It was the most amazing thing we'd ever seen. Some people remarked that it was probably part of a rainbow from an earlier rain, but Jackie and I, and the man behind us too, knew differently. Patty wanted us to know she was okay, and she made sure we arrived home safely too. That was Patty.

We got off the plane and took the escalator down. There was Mario, Malina, Angela, and Aaron. It had been almost two weeks since we'd left, but it had seemed like a lifetime. They were a welcome sight. We got our luggage, and the airport doors opened. Jackie and I walked out those doors into the California sunshine, knowing our lives would never be the same again.

Our family began the process of living without our sister, mom, daughter, aunt, grandma, and friend. We now had a new definition for normal. It would be tough. It would be heartbreaking. It would last forever.

# Conclusion

You've learned a little throughout this book about my relationship with Patty, but there are volumes that will never be written. She mothered me, rocked me, sang to me, and oftentimes wanted to kill me. She was as grounded as could be, and I couldn't get my head out of the clouds to save my ass.

Thank you, Patty, for your unconditional love and understanding. I believe wholeheartedly that you are one of the reasons I've been able to be successful throughout my life. You've encouraged me to stay strong and to have faith. I owe you a tremendous debt, and I hope this book will be a small way for me to keep your memory and spirit alive. You were an inspiration to so many while you were here. My hope is that you'll inspire many more through the pages of this book. You are forever in my heart, my sister, my friend.

On April 6, 2007, my daughter Malina gave birth to my granddaughter, Aliyana Patricia. She is beautiful, smart, and, yes, she is feisty.

On July 4, 2007, Mom died of a heart attack. Well, they said it was a heart attack. We know it was a broken heart.

In early 2008, our sister, Linda, received a kidney transplant after eight years of dialysis. While she's had some difficulty, I know she would call this a complete success.

On December 28, 2009, Dad died of complications from the numerous strokes he'd had. We have all forgiven Dad, and his death was sad for everyone.

www.ingramcontent.com/pod-product-compliance
Lightning Source LLC
Chambersburg PA
CBHW061659120626
46550CB00003B/1013